Road Trips
Michigan Back Roads

by

Ron Rademacher

Revised Edition

Back Roads Publications

P.O. Box 168

Hart, Michigan 49420

PAGE NUMBERS MAP

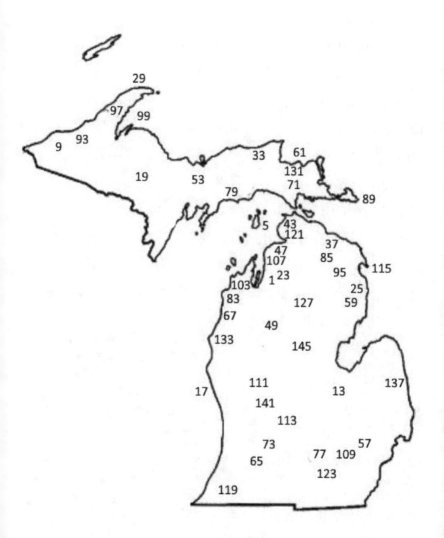

TABLE OF CONTENTS

Road Trips
Michigan Back Roads

by

Ron Rademacher

Back Roads Publication

P.O. Box 168

Hart, Michigan 49420

Acknowledgments

Cover Illustration – Dawn Baumer

Thanks are due to all the people in the small Michigan towns who have made time for my presentations, endless questions, and photographic intrusions.

A special thanks to the shops, businesses and organizations who supported and sponsored this project and to Kathy Jacobs for proof reading.

Road Trips
Michigan Back Roads

by Ron Rademacher

Published by
Back Roads Publications
P.O. Box 168
Hart, Michigan 49420

ISBN: 978-0-9883138-3-5

ALDEN'S MILL HOUSE

Alden, Michigan is the only village, that is directly on the shore, of Torch Lake. Visitors on a scenic drive, around the beautiful lake, might miss one of the most unique shops anywhere in Michigan. Alden is a small village, only a couple of blocks long. As you make the turn, at Torch Lake Drive and Helena, it is easy to drive right by Alden's Mill House. If you love to cook delicious meals and are looking for that extra "something special", the spices created at Alden's Mill House, are just the thing. This shop is so great, that I rarely go through the area, without making it a point to stop in. Especially if I am running low, on their mouth-watering pure ground, roasted garlic.

It all started in 1984, when Eugene Moglovkin, known as Chef Geno, developed his signature all purpose seasoning, "Miracle Blend". That seasoning is just one of the 32+ custom blends, from Pepper Mill Spices, that can turn any cook into a chef. Over the years, Chef Geno developed and perfected his own custom seasoning blends, that have been used in some of America's finest clubs and restaurants. Chef Geno won numerous awards and ribbons, in culinary art shows, from Michigan to Florida. The Pepper Mill, and Alden

Mill House products, are made up of the finest ingredients, carefully chosen from around the world.

The custom blends are one of the reasons these seasonings are so special. Another reason is the attention to quality, that is part of every step in producing each product. The owners use only the highest quality spices from around the world. In addition, they only use kosher flake salt, it has no trace of iodine, that can alter the flavor. They grind and mix all of their spices, label their own bottles, and then fill each bottle individually. The tradition of culinary excellence, started by Chef Geno, is carried on by the family, every day.

There is more. The shop offers cooking utensils, cookbooks, and a fantastic range of gadgets for the kitchen and the grill. Getting into the shop is an experience in itself. From the street is a pathway that meanders through whimsical garden filled with flowers, shrubs, and a whole menagerie of sculptures. On a warm summer day, visitors are welcome to use the benches, and pause in the shade provided by the garden trees. After a rest, head inside and explore the House of Good Taste, Alden's Mill House.

If you go, you could make a day of it. While

enjoying the shopping, and the stunning beauty of Torch Lake, there are a couple of other noteworthy attractions in Alden. The Historical Museum is well worth a visit and has a great view of the lake. If you don't mind a short walk, the Coy Mountain Walking Trail, is a great place to take a break. Located at the corner of Valley Street and Smalley Street, this 11acre natural area, is a hardwood climax forest, that was protected from the timber industry. In 1885, Rueben Coy decided to preserve the forest on this ridge. It became known as Coy Mountain. The trail is only a bit over a mile long. If you take the Long Loop and climb the 170 or so feet to the top, the view of Torch Lake is breathtaking. This small forest is so beautiful that it is worth a special trip during color tour season.

Directions: Alden is on Torch Lake about 1/2 hour north of Kalkaska, and 10 minutes from Bellaire.

PEPPER

HAS BEEN CALLED,

THE KING OF SPICES.

THE BEST KING OF ALL IS

THE ALDEN'S MILL HOUSE

MALABAR ISLAND PEPPER

BEAVER ISLAND

Beaver Island, America's Emerald Isle, is full of history and mystery. It is also home to some of the most pristine natural wilderness anywhere in Michigan. Less developed than some other islands, the Beaver Island Archipelago is remote and rustic, without being primitive. Beaver Island is the largest island in Lake Michigan. It has been home to many peoples and nations, including a unique American religious monarchy, the island is now a popular tourist and vacation destination.

The village of St. James brings to mind a New England fishing village. The main street follows the shore of Paradise Bay. Cool shops like the St. James Boat Shop, museums, and restaurants are here in the downtown. As you stroll the main street you will come across a number of signboards. They tell the remarkable history of the island including King Strang, the arrival of the Irish, Protar the Healer, and the numerous native American nations, that have called Beaver Island home. A visit to the Community Center will provide for maps, directions and WiFi. The community center has information on festivals and events. The Beaver Island Music draws hundreds annually as do the bicycle rallies. Outside of town are more historic sites and natural wonders. Historic sites include two lighthouses, 3 museums, Protar's house and tomb, and the shipwrecks. Plan to see the "Big Rock, a Giant Birch Tree that is a Champion Tree contender, and Little Sand Bay which is part of the Birding Trail. As you travel the island, the Irish influence is all around. Some of the road signs are still in Gaelic.

The Beaver Island Archipelago has been a crossroads of traveling peoples since ancient times. There is evidence of prehistoric occupation on all the islands. Some of the most unusual traces from the past are found in stones. On the west side of Beaver Island below Angeline's Bluff is an enigmatic circle of stones. The construction consists of a circle of glacial boulders that is nearly 400' feet across. While the circle is not constructed of tall, gigantic stones like Stonehenge, it is an important megalithic construction from the prehistoric past of the Great Lakes. The center stone has a hole apparently bored or carved into the center. Several of these stones have markings that have been interpreted as an ancient script. Other carvings appear to be faces. One "face rock" is on display in front of the historical museum downtown. Inside the museum is a photograph of another. Speculations have been made about astronomical alignments of the circle. One theory is that the circle is a calendar device. It takes a bit of tramping around in the forest to get an idea of how big this is. The circle of stones was forgotten, and then was rediscovered in the 1980s.

Direction: From Charlevoix you can get there by Ferry in about 2 1/2 hours. Island Airways can fly you there in about 15 minutes.

NEARLY FORGOTTEN NOW,

CONSTRUCTION OF

THE GRAND HOTEL

ON

MACKINAC ISLAND,

WAS ORIGINALLY BEGUN

ON

BEAVER ISLAND.

BLACK RIVER WATERFALLS

Highway 513, the Black River National Scenic Byway, runs from Route #2 at Bessemer north through the Ottawa National Forest. The road winds along the course of the Black River and is one of two National Scenic Byways in Michigan. At the northern end of the drive, is Lake Superior, and the Black River Harbor, one of only two harbors in the National Forest System. The Harbor is about 15 miles north of Bessemer, and is the location, of the mouth, of the Black River. The section, of the Black River, that flows here, is enclosed by pines, hardwoods, and hemlocks. This section is also graced by several scenic waterfalls that are easy to get to.

The river drops down from the highlands, to Lake Superior. Along the way, the river forms rapids, white water, and four major waterfalls. Parking areas, for each of the major waterfalls, are right off the byway. The waterfalls, in the order you encounter them are, Conglomerate Falls, Potawatomi & Gorge Falls, Sandstone Falls and Rainbow Falls.

It is a hike of nearly a mile along the path from the parking area, to Conglomerate Falls. There is an excellent viewing platform at the river. The waterfall flows over the hard conglomerate riverbed, hence its name, forming a pool, and then a rapids. As with all four waterfalls, the wilderness surrounding adds to the beauty of the scene.

Next is the parking area for the Potawatomi and the Gorge waterfalls. There are picnic facilities at this spot. Potawatomi Falls is the easiest to reach, and has a barrier-free access trail, leading from the parking lot. Gorge Falls is 400 feet from the parking area, and you will have to deal with long stairways. It is worth it. Gorge falls is in a steep gorge, carved by the river, and is a photographers' dream.

Sandstone Falls is next. The sign says it is a quarter mile from the parking area, to the waterfall. It doesn't mention that most of that is a steep stairway. The Sandstone waterfall is completely different from the others. It is in a broad, flat section of the river, and it is possible to walk out onto the riverbed in late summer. The area is wild and rugged, and the view is reminiscent of scenes, of the high country out west.

Finally, we reach Rainbow Falls. Getting to the river, requires the usual hike, and the usual stairs. The roaring waterfall plunges into a deep, dark crater. The drop is sufficient, to throw great quantities of mist into the air. When the sun is at the correct angle, gorgeous waterfalls form spontaneously, only to disappear in the wind.

After visiting all the waterfalls, it is just a short drive to the mouth of the river and the Black River Harbor. This area has plenty of parking, a spacious picnic area, and a foot bridge across the river to the shoreline. The scenery is beautiful, making this a perfect spot for a picnic, and a rest, after climbing up and down to the waterfalls.

Directions: The Black River National Scenic Byway, begins on County Road 513, at its intersection with County Road 204 (Airport Road), and runs north for 11 miles. Route 513, leads north, from Bessemer, which is about 7 or 8 miles east of Wisconsin, and about 60 miles from Ontonagon, at the east end of the Porcupine Mountains.

THIS SECTION

OF

HIGHWAY 513

WAS DESIGNATED

A

NATIONAL FOREST SCENIC BYWAY

IN

1992

CHESANING BRIDGE DISASTER

Not all historic events took place long, long ago. In the winters of 2008, and again in 2009, the Shiawassee River at Chesaning, demonstrated the awesome power of Michigan winters. Chesaning, Michigan is an historic town located in the center of Saginaw County. Situated on the banks of the Shiawassee River, the history of town and river have been linked, since the area was first settled. This community has always taken a genuine interest in preserving local history, and it was with great pride that they purchased a truss bridge slated for demolition, from a nearby town. At great expense, the entire structure was moved to Cole Park. The bridge was installed on foundations just downstream from the dam, to link the foot path on each bank.

Everyone applauded the spirit of preservation and agreed that the bridge, one of only three in the U.S., was a genuine treasure and a crown jewel, of the foot path. The whole community was set to enjoy the picturesque bridge crossing that was so unique to the town and park. As autumn came to an end and winter approached, no one anticipated that it would be any different from any other, nor the amazing event that was about to take place. The river froze which was not that unusual. Ice began to build up and push on the old dam. This was of no great concern. The town was planning to demolish the dam and replace it with a modern weir anyway. If the ice build up helped that process, so much the better, but there was trouble coming as Mother Nature rolled up her sleeves, spit on her hands, and got down to it. The ice continued to build up, and stack up, and stack up some more, until it was high enough to reach the bridge, which was way up in the air, I mean way up. Then, incredibly, the ice lifted the newly moved bridge right off its foundations. The weather got colder and the ice kept coming and finally the river won. The beautiful historic bridge was dumped into the river and was completely wrecked.

The old dam has been replaced with a modern weir that produces super rapids to the delight of kayak and canoe enthusiasts. Cole Park continues to develop, and all of this is just downstream from Showboat Park. The old, wrecked bridge has been removed from the river. A visit to the Chesaning Historical Museum will be worth the effort. They have photos of how the bridge was brought to town and installed. The museum, downtown, also has information about the Showboat. It was a paddle wheeler that operated on the river during festivals. It was demolished and is another treasure lost to history.

Directions: Chesaning, Michigan, is an hour and half northwest of Detroit on Route 57. The river flows right through downtown.

CHESANING

CHI-ASIN

MEANS

PLACE

OF THE

BIG ROCK

CLEANEST BEACH IN MICHIGAN

Michigan has more fresh water coastline than any other state in the union. In the lower peninsula, you are never more than 85 miles from one of the great lakes, and day trips to the lakes are a favorite getaway. Whether for sun bathing, hunting agates, or splashing about in the sparkling water, everyone has their favorite beach, but Muskegon has the cleanest beach.

The Pere' Marquette Beach, on the shores of Lake Michigan, and adjoining the Muskegon Lake Channel, is the only nationally certified "Clean Beach", on the Great Lakes. There are miles of beach to wander, and there are those famous Lake Michigan sunsets. The public beach and park are owned by the City of Muskegon and cover some 27 acres. Possibly one of the best kept secrets in Muskegon County, the park includes a number of play areas, sand volleyball courts, and well-kept picnic and sunbathing areas. Add in the recently improved bike trail and over 200 feet of paved handicap-accessible walkways, and you have all the amenities needed to enjoy a getaway to the cleanest beach in Michigan.

A day at the beach could include a little site seeing. The Pier Head Lighthouse is a vintage 53-foot historic structure built in 1851. Take U.S. 31

to Muskegon and Sherman Boulevard. Take Sherman to Beach St. and Beach St. to the pier. Downtown Muskegon is rich with historic architecture including several Victorian era mansions. You can visit three World War II ships, including the USS Silversides, a real submarine berthed along the channel wall at Pere' Marquette Park adjoining the maritime museum.

Directions: From U.S. 31 take the Laketon Ave. exit and head west. Laketon becomes Lakeshore Dr. which will eventually intersect with the beach. The beach is at the northern end of city-owned Lake Michigan frontage that runs for over two miles.

CRYSTAL FALLS

Crystal Falls is an historic city in the western upper peninsula and is the county seat of Iron County. It doesn't matter from which direction one approaches Crystal Falls. On the highest point sits the magnificent County Courthouse. That building nearly didn't end up here. In the 1800s, Iron River had been designated the temporary County Seat, but Crystal Falls had other ideas. The actual county seat was to be determined in the upcoming election and both towns wanted the honor. The "Stealing of the Courthouse" has been the topic of many a conversation and article. It wasn't the actual courthouse that was stolen, it was the county records, that are housed at the county seat. It is somewhat difficult to separate fact from fiction. Most versions of the story agree that a poker game was arranged, to follow a board of supervisors meeting, in the temporary courthouse in Iron River.

The game was at its height at the Old Boyington Hotel. The game was another competition between the two communities. Most of the residents of Iron River were on hand to watch. Two Crystal Falls men, Frank Scadden and Bert

Hughitt, left the game pretending to go upstairs to bed. Instead, they snuck out, and back to the temporary courthouse. Treasurer Hughitt cleared the safe of all county records, loaded them on a sled, and took them to the rail yard where they were loaded into a boxcar. The two men took the records to Stager, the oldest station in the County, and then they were put into safe keeping – some say in hollow pine trees, others in the Mastodon Mine.

Election time came and the voting was fevered. Lumberjacks from surrounding counties were brought in by both towns to help with the voting. Enthusiasm ran so high that even residents of local cemeteries managed to cast their votes. Ultimately, Crystal Falls won the election by 5 votes and became the county seat. Not willing to leave well enough alone. The town fathers decided they needed a new courthouse and built one of the finest in the upper peninsula. As soon as you arrive the historic courthouse is the dominant building you will see. All of the records of the "theft" are on display, along with dozens of other interesting exhibits.

It is easy to spend a couple days finding all the hidden treasures in and around Crystal Falls. First off, there is no waterfall called Crystal Falls.

There is the cascade formed by the dam on the Painted River, but that was never a falls. The closest thing to a famous waterfall nearby is Horserace Rapids. It is just a few miles south of town. This rapids is popular with paddlers. During the spring thaw it becomes a roaring white water. At that time of year, only the skilled and the foolish challenge the gorge.

One of the genuine treasures in town is inside the Crystal Theatre. They have the distinction of possessing the largest theatre pipe organ in Michigan's Upper Peninsula. The organ, consisting of 3 manuals (keyboards) and 21 ranks, (sets of pipes) was originally built in 1927 by the M.P. Möller Company of Hagerstown, Maryland. There are more than 1,600 pipes, installed in the on-stage chambers, ranging in size from half an inch to over 16 feet in length.

Then there is the world famous Humongous Fungus. Covering over 37 acres and weighing in at more than 100 tons, it was once the oldest living organism on earth. Every summer, Crystal Falls celebrates their famous resident with the Humongous Fungus Festival.

THE CASPIAN

HISTORICAL MUSEUM

HOUSES

EXTREMELY RARE

ARTIFACTS

INCLUDING

STILLS

FROM THE

RUM REBELLION

DEADMAN'S HILL

Driving along Highway 131, in Antrim County, watch for a small brown sign announcing Deadman's Hill. The designated road leads to an overlook, Deadman's Hill, that provides a spectacular view of the steep forested hills that form the Jordan River Valley. From the parking area there is a short hike uphill to the overlook. A split rail fence is provided as a safety measure, it is a very steep drop. There is also a path along the fence that allows you to get to different spots to enjoy the vista. The view is gorgeous during color time, with wave after wave of flaming hardwoods, and the river sparkling below.

This beautiful spot got its name from a tragedy. Logging the great forests was a dangerous business, particularly in the steep hills of the Jordan River Valley. One fatal accident was the death of Stanley Graczyk, known as "Big Sam". Only 21 years of age, he was killed while driving a team of horses and big wheels loaded with logs. As he headed down the steep trail, he somehow fell beneath the wheel. "Big Sam's" final resting place is in Elmira's St. Thomas's Churchyard.

If you want to get a closer look at the Jordan River there is an 18 mile loop that begins at Deadman's Hill. Another way is to visit the nearby Jordan River National Fish Hatchery. The hatchery produces over 3 million trout every year. Visitors can see all the stages of growth from egg to trophy sized brown trout. In addition to the fish, there are picnic facilities and access to miles of trails, and the river. This is one of the easiest ways to access the river during the winter months. The Jordan River was Michigan's first National Wild and Scenic River.

Directions to the hatchery: From Gaylord, Michigan: Take state highway M-32 west to junction of highway US-131, (13.0 mi.) Turn left onto US-131, travel 4.0 miles to Turner Road. Take right on Turner Road, travel 1.9 miles to hatchery.

DINOSAUR GARDENS

In the summer of 1935, Paul Domke began work in the small town of Ossineke, on what would become a world famous project, the Dinosaur Gardens - Ossineke's Prehistoric Zoo. Mr. Domke had searched for just the right spot for his project. He wanted a spot that would recreate an authentic environment for the giant sculptures he planned to create. He searched for a spot that could represent the environment, as it was in prehistoric periods when dinosaurs flew through the air and grazed near the great inland seas.

After years of research in both northern Michigan and Canada, he chose a cedar lowland with huge ferns, majestic cedars, and the Devils River meandering through, at Ossineke, Michigan, on the shores of Lake Huron. Mr. Domke and his crew built a bridge over the river, they constructed a 1/2 mile trail through the wilderness, and prepared picturesque spots to showcase the sculptures, that were still on the drawing board. The first display was started in 1935 and later finished in 1936. Mr. Domke even had to invent a special cement formulation, that could withstand the elements, and yet be pliable enough to show the details he wanted in each piece. During the years of artistic creation, every effort was made to preserve the natural state of the park environment.

When you get just a little way into the park, you will see that those efforts paid off. It is easy to imagine that you have been transported back in time. Along the trail you will find depictions of an iguanadon, a velocirapter, an ongoing struggle in a tar pit, a stegosaurus and many more. If you look closely, there is even a dinosaur fish sculpture in the river, near the bridge. The gardens include about 20 acres. In addition to the enormous sculptures, wildflowers abound, giant ferns grow among the cedar trees. On the ridge there are White Pines, Norway Pines, and Hemlock trees.

The Dinosaur Gardens required nearly forty years to create and contains over 25 life-size dinosaurs, from various periods of history. Many of the attractions of this kind, that were created from the 1930's to the 1950's, have been lost. This one has been preserved and maintained and is still in operation today. Even the bridge over the Devils River is still there. The pathway wanders through the cedars, and the dinosaurs are revealed, as you hike through the ferns and trees. The workmanship on the displays is remarkable, and the settings are very realistic. Adult visitors say they feel like little kids again, as they wander through the gardens.

Directions: The Dinosaur Gardens are on the U.S. 23 Heritage Route, in Alpena County. Existing exhibits are being renovated and new exhibits may be added in the coming years. There is a gift shop, ice cream shop, and miniature golf on the property.

OSSINEKE

DERIVES FROM AN

ANISHINAABE WORD

MEANING

"WHERE

THE

IMAGE STONES

STOOD"

ESTIVANT PINES

I was first drawn to the Estivant Pines by stories of a legendary fallen giant pine, the former Michigan champion white pine. The Estivant Pines Nature Sanctuary, is a 377-acre stand of old growth Eastern White Pine, growing in a mixed hardwood forest. Comparisons have been made with other places in the upper peninsula, such as, the Porcupine Mountains or the Huron Mountains. The major differences are that this place is a bit wilder and, these white pines are really old. Some are more than six hundred years old. This sanctuary is also home to the "fallen giant", formerly the champion white pine.

As soon as you leave the parking area, you will enter a place. There are no improvements here and the going can be rugged. Even people in good shape have found these trails to be a handful. The sanctuary is a beautiful place, and you may want to linger a while. Dress appropriately and take water with you. This is a wild spot with no facilities other than a privy. Leaving the trail is risky even for the experienced and well equipped. This is rugged terrain. The trails often have roots protruding out of them. In several places there are rudimentary boardwalks for crossing wet areas. Those caveats noted, this is a beautiful wilderness full of silence with lush growth, and it is usually devoid of crowds. Then there is the forest itself which is not all pines. There are a lot of old hardwoods as well, with the stands of old growth pines scattered throughout.

A short distance in, a sign describes the loop options. The two main loops form a sort of figure rough 'eight'. Each loop is about a mile long and both the Cathedral Grove loop and the Memorial Grove loop leads to awesome stands of the ancient pines. There are several distinctive trees found in the sanctuary. Along the way is a pine with a hollow trunk and in another spot is a pair of pines known as the "Twins". One can easily spend a lot of time in this forest. It is important to remember that there are no facilities inside the sanctuary. Bring water and energy bars, at a minimum, if you plan to spend time walking both loops. There are, after all, nearly 400 acres of pristine forest.

Then there is the sign that announces the "Fallen Giant Trail". It describes the trail as a swampy hike, recommended only for experienced hikers with proper gear; believe it. If you are looking for something "off the beaten path", this is it. Hiking the side trail toward the "fallen giant" is worth it, just to see the cedar swamp that blocks the way.

Hundreds and hundreds of fallen tree trunks are scattered in every direction. The one time I attempted to cross the swamp, the water was quite deep. I left my companion, Helga, on the edge of the swamp and made my way in, moving from tree to tree. Balancing on the dead fall, the going was treacherous at best. There is no trail through the swamp, just trees, water, and underbrush. When I reached a point where I was going to lose sight of Helga, there was nothing but swamp and fallen trees in every direction. It was primeval. I decided that going further alone and without proper preparation was foolish. It was discouraging, but the smart decision was to turn back. The "fallen giant" remains on my list. Helga still tells the story of how I left her in the wilderness surrounded by the growls of huge bears and howling wolves in search of some old tree that had fallen.

DIRECTIONS:

Just go through Copper Harbor and follow the signs. Parking is gravel.

THE

ESTIVANT PINES

ARE

OLD

GROWTH,

SOME

ARE

600 YEARS

OLD

FIFTY MILES OF HEAVEN

For years, one of the most beautiful drives in the upper peninsula of Michigan, was also one of the roughest. H-58 is a two-lane road, that runs from Grand Marais to Munising. Until that road was paved a few years ago, the route was so rough that travelers using motorcycles, RV's, and sports cars avoided the winding gravel roadway. Consequently, they missed out on a gorgeous scenic drive through quiet forests, with awesome views of the dunes, and Lake Superior. Now that the roadway has been paved, the route we have always called "Fifty Miles of Heaven", is smooth and safe for every kind of vehicle.

Choosing a starting point depends on plans for what to do at each end. One can begin this scenic drive from either Munising or Grand Marais. For example, Munising at the west end of the route, is home to a world famous destination, the Pictured Rocks. If you plan to take a commercial boat tour, you will need about three hours just for that. At the east end of the route, Grand Marais offers a charming downtown, a museum shaped like a pickle barrel, and the Dunes Saloon/Lake Superior Brewing Company where they still serve those mouth-watering scotch eggs.
There are spectacular views, and overlooks of

Lake Superior, wilderness trails, and historic stops. Here are some of the features along the way. There are lots of places to pause, explore, and enjoy.

Starting from Grand Marais, the first stop, Sable Falls, is just outside of town. The parking is good and the trail to the falls is well maintained. There are some stairs to deal with if you want the best view of the waterfall. Making your way to the lower viewing area is well worth it. This is a fairly tall, cascading waterfall that is perfect for picture taking.

The old log slide is next. Since the forest roads could be impassable, the lumbermen would slide logs down this steep slope and into Lake Superior. This was a dangerous activity. The logs would plunge hundreds of feet down the sand cliffs into the freezing waters. More than one lumberjack lost his life at this work. After the timber was in the lake, the logs could be loaded onto ships, and transported to the sawmills. The actual log slide is long gone, but the beautiful Grand Sable Dunes, where the log slide once was, provide stunning views of the lake.

The White Birch Forest can be found about 15-16 miles west of Grand Marais. This picturesque stand of white birch is unique in this part of the upper peninsula. Hikers can take advantage of a two-mile long, self-guiding interpretive trail, that begins at the east end of Twelve Mile Campground. The trail meanders through the beautiful white birch trees and explores the natural history of the nearby uplands. This environment is quite different from the nearby dunes on Lake Superior.

Another pristine area is the Beaver Basin Wilderness. The wilderness includes 13 miles of Lake Superior shoreline encompassing Seven Mile Creek and Spray Falls. The wilderness runs inland from Lake Superior for about 3.5 miles. In all there are more than 11,000 acres of woodlands, lakes, and streams. The North Country Trail runs through here along with a number of connector trails. There is quiet and solitude, to enjoy and refresh, before moving on.

The famous Miners Castle rock formation is only about 6 or 7 miles east of Munising. This is one of the most photographed rock formations in the entire Pictured Rocks National Lakeshore. Take Miners Castle Road north about 5 miles from H-58. There are excellent trails and overlook platforms. The comfort facilities are only open in the summer months.

At the Munising end of the drive there are several waterfalls that are easily accessible like Wagner Falls, with its several levels of plunging waters, and tiny Scott Falls west of town. The famous Laughing White Fish waterfall is a few miles outside of town. The falls at Mosquito Beach forms a natural water slide that drops into Lake Superior.

Nearly all of the H-58 drive runs along the Pictured Rocks National Lakeshore. These soaring cliffs display vibrant colors and various formations including towers, arches and waterfalls. To appreciate the beauty of these majestic cliffs, you really need to be out on the water. There are a number of options for getting out on Lake Superior to tour the 200' high cliffs. A kayak will do it, or a pontoon boat, or you can take one of the local tours that are offered.

FORTY MILE POINT LIGHTHOUSE

The 40 Mile Point Lighthouse is unique for how it was built, for the rare lens that sends out the light and for the shipwreck that is in the shallows just offshore. These and other features are good reasons for putting this lighthouse on your getaway list. The main building has been faithfully restored. The white ash woodwork and floors are there. Period items make up the furnishings and provide a realistic sense of what life was like for the lighthouse keepers. The guided tour is entertaining, informative and will provide all the details and secrets that aren't included in this brief chapter.

Operating the light was no small matter, kerosene had to be replenished, firewood had to be gathered, cut and split, and fuel for the foghorn boilers had to be maintained. The light lens rotated by way of weights powered by a clockwork mechanism. That clockwork mechanism had to be rewound about every 2-4 hours, depending on the ambient temperature, all night. The kerosene lamp needed constant attention. In the keeper's quarters there is a skylight that. That skylight acted as an alarm for the light housekeeper. If the kerosene lamp up above went out, no light would come down through the skylight so the keeper would be alerted and could dash up there to ignite the lantern. During a big storm when Mother Nature got really serious it could seem like it was just one thing after another.

Construction of the lighthouse and other buildings on the grounds began in 1896. The conditions under which that construction took place were difficult at best, given the wilderness, weather and the equipment that was available. Some equipment simply wasn't available, like power tools and electricity. The way it was done is hard to imagine a hundred years later. 17 men and women were dropped into the wilderness on the shore of Lake Huron. They were isolated the entire time, no roads in or out. All the supplies necessary to sustain the group had been off loaded at the same time the men landed. Four months later they had built the lighthouse, an amazing achievement. Even more astonishing is that they built the lighthouse twice. The brick walls that are visible are actually outer walls. There are identical inner walls separated from the outer by 4 inches of air. The air layer acts as insulation. There is more. These guys also erected a building to hold fuel, lightkeepers living quarters and a separate building to house the foghorns. They also built a small railroad used to move all those supplies and building materials around the grounds.

The light at the top of the tower was the whole point. At the time of construction, the light source was a simple lantern that burned kerosene. The Fresnel Lens was the miraculous apparatus that projected that light to a point 16 miles out into the darkness of Lake Huron. At this writing the 40 Mile Point lighthouse has the only operating 4th order Fresnel Lens on Lake Huron. The Fresnel Lens was a revolutionary development and was the most efficient light mechanism until the development of the laser. The originals were from France, made of crystal. A fourth order lens concentrates up to 87% of the light from the source on the distant point of focus. The lens weighed 300 pounds and a clock work mechanism with a counterweight would make the lens rotate creating the effect of a beam of light sweeping across the night sky. Eventually it was figured out how to rotate a metal cutout inside the lens instead of rotating the whole works. The lens was constructed to focus the beacon on a point 16 miles from shore, though that can be affected by the curve of the earth. This light is 52 feet above lake level, the light can be seen 10 miles out at lake level and 14 miles out from the upper deck of a modern "laker". Each lighthouse on the Great Lakes has its own timing, so you can determine where you are by the timing of the light you are observing. Currently, this beacon flashes in three second intervals.

Oddly, there are conditions under which the light can be seen 100 miles away, in Canada. Those conditions are known as "ice lensing". Under the correct atmospheric conditions of water vapor, temperature and ice crystals, light from the lens can bounce or skip from ice crystal to ice crystal all the way across the lake. This effect is similar to the phenomenon of whole cities appearing on the distant horizon high in the sky.

There is a walking trail along the Lake Huron shoreline known as the "Shipwreck" trail. The trailhead is just down from the lighthouse. At the other end is part of the wreck of the schooner, Joseph S. Fay. The entry in the lighthouse keeper's logbook for October 20, 1905 tells part of the story. "At 8:30 p.m. last night the steamer, J. S. Fay, came ashore here in a sinking condition. She soon broke up. Most of the crew came ashore on the Pilot House. Three men swam ashore, the mate was drowned." The entry for December 4, 1905 reads: "The assistant found a dead man on the beach about 1 mile up. We think it is the mate of the Fay." The Rhodes was being towed by the wooden steamer Joseph S. Fay loaded with iron ore. Caught in one of those legendary Lake Huron storms, the Fay ran aground and broke up. The Rhodes drifted on for a while and ran aground near the light house. The lighthouse gift shop has all the history about the wreck and other events at the 40 Mile Point.

GOOD HART

IS

HALF

WAY

ALONG

THE

TUNNEL

OF

TREES

GOOD HART GENERAL STORE

Highway M-119 hugs the Lake Michigan coastline from Harbor Springs to Cross Village in the far northwest of Michigan's lower peninsula. The road winds through a hardwood forest. The branches of the trees arch across the road forming a roof of living green so it has become known as the Tunnel of Trees. The drive through the trees is stunningly beautiful in all seasons. 137 curves in 20 miles winding along Lake Michigan make for a leisurely pace. Along the way visitors encounter historic places like the Old Council Tree and the Devil's Elbow. Signs at these spots explain how it was named or describe historic events that occurred there. At the south end, Harbor Springs is a popular resort area. At the north end one finds Cross Village and the Legs Inn where Polish cuisine is the specialty. About mid-way is the town of Good Hart and the general store.

When giving directions people often say, "You can't miss it", which usually means you will drive right by it, missing it completely. In the case of the Good Hart General Store, don't worry, you can't miss it. It is painted a bright red, and on any summer weekend, there are usually crowds of smiling people hanging around. Just park along the road like everyone else has and get ready for some fun.

The store serves as the Good Hart post office, so it has become a meeting place for summer residents to reconnect after wintering in the south. It is a genuine general store with supplies, groceries and locally produced gifts, jams and jellies. They also have an excellent deli serving up delicious meals, desserts and ice cream. Then there are those incredible potpies. They offer chicken and beef in large and small. These are the best potpies I have found anywhere in Michigan. It wouldn't surprise me if they are the best in the world. These potpies are so good you may not want one from anywhere else ever again. That won't be a problem, the Good Hart General Store will ship them in dry ice anywhere and it is worth it. On the weekends a lot of the action is outside where events are staged. There is a shady glade next to the store and something is going on there on nearly any weekend. Local growers set up a small farmers market. Artists and crafters set up booths and musicians sometimes stop by for impromptu performances. There are picnic tables among the trees and people just seem to gather here and enjoy whatever is going on.

There are a couple of other attractions in the immediate area. Just a bit north is a small sign pointing to the St. Ignatius Church. Originally established in 1741, the restored church is open for tours including a Native American burial ground. South of Good Hart is the Thorne Swift Nature Preserve. There is only a small sign to let you know this natural wonderland is there, so this is one that you can miss. Three trails totaling 1 ¼ miles are well maintained and offer a nice stroll through the woodlands or down to a smooth stone-filled shore on Lake Michigan. The trails are comfortable and include boardwalks where necessary.

THE

CHARLEVOIX

HISTORICAL MUSEUM

HAS A

HEMINGWAY

MARRIAGE LICENSE

ON

DISPLAY

HEMINGWAY COUNTRY

Northern Michigan has become a destination for vacationers from all over. In the northwest region the Leelanau peninsula, Empire, and Port Oneida along with the Cherry Festival are just a few of the attractions. One area that is often overlooked is locally known as Hemingway Country. Hemingway country is roughly an area defined by a triangle marked by Boyne City, Charlevoix and Petoskey. The area left an impression on Ernest Hemingway and inspired two of his books, "Up In Michigan" and "Big Two Hearted River". You can still walk the trails that Hemingway loved, the cottage of Windemere is still there at Walloon Lake, though it isn't open to the public.

The center of "Hemingway Country" is the village of Horton Bay, a few miles west of Boyne City, on C-56. The Horton Bay General Store is good for food and supplies during the season. Next to that is the Red Fox Inn. If you drive by you are missing a real "up north" treat. There is a log cabin and other historic buildings on the grounds. The inn has a small gift shop featuring books and photos of the area. The original owner of the Red Fox was a genuine Michigan character and author. When he was alive, no one was known to have entered the gift shop, and gotten out without buying something. Just west of town you will find Horton's Creek, where Ernest Hemingway enjoyed trout fishing.

There are a number of hidden treasures in this area that make for a cool day trip. Walloon Lake is probably the most famous "Hemingway" destination. A few miles west of Horton Bay is the historic Greensky Hill Mission and Native American burial ground. The sign is rather small, so it is easy to miss. Adjacent to the church property is an ancient council site. If you look carefully, you can see several huge maple trees, with twisted branches, standing in a circle. The circle is no longer complete as one of the old trees has fallen. This circle was a council site for the tribes native to this area.

Lake Charlevoix is the main feature of the area. A walk along the beach near Young's State Park may bring you to the "tourist-made" inverted forest. Years of visitors have retrieved fallen trees and "planted" them upside down in the shallow water. There are so many upside down trees that the inverted forest is even visible from the other side of Lake Charlevoix. On the north side of Lake Charlevoix is the Ironton Ferry. It is great fun, holds about 4 cars total. The ride across the water takes about 2 minutes.

HIDDEN FALLS - LOWER PENINSULA

There are dozens of waterfalls in the upper peninsula of Michigan. Some are breath-taking, like Canyon Falls, and some might be better described as rapids. Some folks think there is just one in the lower peninsula and some folks swear there are two. In fact, there are at least three waterfalls in the lower peninsula of Michigan, if you include Ocqueoc Falls. To visit this unnamed waterfall you have to drive into the heart of the Manistee National Forest. You are going to take a couple of gravel roads and then a short hike through the forest to the waterfall that plunges into the Manistee River. You can picnic, or camp, on a bluff overlooking the falls and the river. It is important to note that the trail to the falls is a bit rough, and quite steep in places, so dress appropriately, especially if you go in winter.

There are a number of ways to find this waterfall. Hikers on the North Country Trail will come across it near the suspension bridge. Then there are the two sets of directions below which will get you there. After following the first directions below, you will be at the Hodenpyl Dam. You could cross the river at this spot on the suspension foot bridge and get to the North Country Trail. The dam creates the Hodenpyl Pond, and the falls are downstream, a couple of miles from here. Now you make the decision to walk along the trails, or drive further into the forest, as described in the second directions.

First directions: Get onto Route 37. This is an excellent paved two lane that intersects 10 in Baldwin. Head out of Baldwin and make for Mesick about 30 miles north. A few miles south of Mesick you want to take NO 26 RD and head west. This is gravel so go easy as it can be a bit rough. Stay on the road and follow it around as it curves to the right. There are other roads branching off, but if you stay on this, you will get to the dam and parking area. Now you park and walk or take the second part of the drive.

Second directions: From the dam turn left onto the two track "snake trail" that heads into the forest, go slow. This two-track will branch often, and every time it does, you want to keep to the right. Keep going, branching right, and after a while you will see a metal gate on your right. The last time I was there it was painted brown. This is the first gate you will have come to.

Park in any of the rough parking spots, there are 4 or 5 available, and walk around the gate. Go back to your car and get your camera. Walk around the gate. Go back to your car and get your water.

Walk around the gate. After a few annoying treks back to your car for other stuff, head down the trail that starts here. In a few moments you will hear only the birds and the wind in the trees. 600 – 700 yards down the trail you will arrive at the river and the waterfall.

Waterfall Notes: There are, in fact, at least two other waterfalls in the lower peninsula. One is Ocqueoc Falls in Presque Isle County. Another is in southwest Michigan outside Bear Cave.

THERE

IS AN

UNDERGROUND

RIVER

NEAR

OCQUEOC

FALLS

HIDDEN FALLS – UPPER PENINSULA

This is a fun day trip that will take you to five waterfalls in one afternoon. The waterfalls include Wagner Falls, Scott Falls, Laughing Whitefish Falls, Alger Falls, and a small waterfall that isn't on any map I've seen. A couple of the falls can be seen without getting out of your car and all of them are very accessible. There are a number of ways to take this drive depending on your starting point. Gladstone on Bay de Noc is one of my favorites. There are picnic spots on this trip, so pack some treats or pick up some Trenary Toast. Trenary is a tiny village noted for Outhouse Races and murals. Also in town is the bakery that makes Trenary Toast. Ask around at the small markets you find. Packaged in brown paper bags this stuff is incredible, especially if you dunk it in coffee for breakfast.

Starting from Gladstone, we went north on 41 to Trenary where you catch 67 going north. A few miles on, you will come to 94 where you will turn right. Remember this junction, because the secret waterfall is nearby, and we will be coming back this way. Just 16 miles further and you come to Highway 28 near Munising. Alger Falls is at that junction. Turn around, head back and park at the pull off. A short stroll up a well tended path will bring you to Wagner Falls, a beautiful waterfall that fills the air with music. After a few minutes at the waterfall, you will want to dash back to your car, and start reading this swell book again. Head toward Munising. The road pretty much follows the shore of Lake Superior and you can see Grand Island in the distance. Stay on 28 for a few miles. Just west of Munising, is tiny Scott Falls on the left. On the right side of the road is a park where you can stop and take pictures.

Continuing west, watch for a road named H-03 near Au Train, where you will turn left. This is an improved road, but take it slow, allow yourself to enjoy the gorgeous forest. You could have turned right, but it is very wet that way. Keep heading south on H-03 for 4 or 5 miles and you will arrive back at 94. Go west, that is a right turn, and in 4 miles you will be at the junction of 94 & 67 again; the junction I said you should remember. Turn right, that is north, and drive toward Chatham. Go easy since you will pull off the road quite soon.

Rolling north toward Chatham, you will see a rather small municipal park on the left-hand side of the road. There is an enormous snow-roller there, and a couple of one-holers, for the convenience of travelers and those on a picnic. In fact, this is one of the great spots for a picnic on this drive. The park is enclosed by a split rail fence. At the back of the park is an archway with a path leading into the trees. Hike down that path a bit, you will come to a small waterfall that isn't on any map. It is in a small clearing about a five minute walk in and you will hear it before you see it. No, it isn't a thundering cataract like Canyon Falls, but it is a tranquil spot visited by few.

Back on the road, you head north into Chatham and follow 94 west again. Seven miles down the road you will come to Sundell, Michigan. Watch for the sign telling you to turn north to reach Laughing Whitefish Falls. This is a famous waterfall, and it is only a couple of miles to the parking area. The road was a bit dicey last time I went. After parking you will have to walk about a mile, but the path is not bad, and the waterfall is worth every step of it. We explored for an hour and had a great time; no one else was there.

We are in the car again and are back at 94 heading west again. In about 7 miles you will come to 41 again. If you turn south here, you will be back in Gladstone in less than an hour. If you turn north instead, there is a very pretty drive. Follow 94 as it meanders north and west until you come to 553. Take 553 south about 5 miles and you will come to 35. Turn right toward Gwinn and stay on 35 for about 15 miles. The road twists and turns all over, so drive carefully. Up towards Palmer you will find Warner Falls which can be seen from the road. A bit further on is the National Mine near Ishpeming. You have to see the site to believe it. When you have had enough just follow 35 south and you will get back to Gladstone.

HORSE COUNTRY

About forty-five minutes north of Detroit, and about 90 miles east of Lansing, you can enter a world of white painted fences, champion stallions, and broad rolling horse farms. In that short drive, you will leave the noise and clamor behind, and enjoy a quiet relaxing day, in Metamora, Michigan. If you look up the word "quaint", in the dictionary, you may see a picture of Metamora. Make your way to Route 24 in Lapeer County and discover the beauty of a day in horse country.

The White Horse Inn is still here. It was the oldest continuously operating restaurant in Michigan for more than 125 years. Now under new ownership, it is still one of the most popular dining spots in the entire region. No word yet if the resident ghost still haunts the premises.

A visit to Metamora at the right time of summer will get you there while their Hot Air Balloon Jamboree is in full swing. At holiday time don't be surprised to see horse-drawn sleighs taking folks around, to see the Christmas light decorations. This is not make believe horse country. There are real professionals at work here. The Metamora Hunt is a high point of the season. The spectacle of the red-clad riders cantering, with the hounds in full voice, will take you back in time.

Directions for the Horse Country Drive: After exploring downtown, a leisurely drive on the country roads is just the thing. From the center of town go east on Dryden until you come to Barber Road. Go south to Brocker. At this point you can turn west, or continue on to Rock Valley Road, and then turn west there. Travel west until you come to Blood Road, then turn north again and make your way back to town. Essentially it is a big circle. All the way you are cruising through the broad meadows and fields of Metamora's horse country. Beautiful horses, well-kept buildings, and stunning homes are on every side. It is easy to understand how the Metamora Hunt has continued to grow here. It is also easy to forget, that downtown Detroit is less than an hour away.

IARGO SPRINGS

At the base of a bluff, near the Au Sable River, pure water flows out of the ground, at a place known as Iargo Springs. Large pools have formed, one is more than 50 feet across, and the waters are crystal clear. So clear, in fact, that it is difficult to judge the actual depth. The pathway is well maintained, and there are boardwalks, that make it easy to wander through the quiet forest. Small wooden bridges cross the streams formed, as the spring waters flow out of the earth. This was considered a sacred place, by native peoples, and it is easy to understand why. The solitude here is magical. Along with the pure water, and the views across the wetlands, the only sounds you are likely to hear, are the wind, and the cries of eagles.

Getting there is fun as well, since it entails a scenic drive, along the River Road Scenic Byway. This scenic byway, one of two in Michigan, winds along the course of the Au Sable River, from Oscoda on Lake Huron, west to Route 65. Keep a sharp eye out as you go. The scenery is beautiful, but the sign to Iargo Springs is small. You may be puzzled when you first arrive. All you see is a parking lot, a sign stating that you are at the Iargo Springs interpretive site, and there is a kiosk with some photos, but no springs in sight.

Near the kiosk, is a scenic overlook, offering a stunning view of the Au Sable River. At that point, you will find the boardwalk and stairs, leading to the sacred springs. Be warned, there are about 300 stairs to descend, to get to the springs, and that means a long climb back up. The tranquility and beauty of the springs, make it worth it. The climb is made more enjoyable, by benches where you can pause and rest. At the bottom of the steps the pathway and boardwalk lead to the springs.

This can turn into a full day trip, as there are a number of other attractions, in the immediate area. Just south of Iargo Springs, is the Lumberman's Monument, which includes an excellent museum and educational programs. There are scenic turnouts all along the River Road.

IROQUOIS POINT

Iroquois Point is found along the Whitefish Bay Scenic Byway, about 20 miles west of Sault Ste. Marie. The "point" has become a popular stop along the byway due to the lighthouse that stands there. There are 72 steps to the top, open to climb in the summer months, where the fourth order Fresnel lens was housed. That lens was powerful enough to send a beam of light sixteen miles out into the night. As you watch one of the gigantic lake freighters making way on Lake Superior, the importance of this point of land and the light station become clear.

The light isn't functional and the tower serves as a museum. The guiding light is now provided by an automatic facility at Gros Cap, Ontario. The museum is more than a tower and stairs to the top. Pictures, tools of the trade, and antique furniture tell the story of the day-to-day life of the lighthouse keepers and their families. The museum has faithfully restored the lighthouse assistants' apartment to its 1950's condition. It is like stepping back in time. The museum also operates a book shop stocked with historical great lakes selections. Close by is the access to the beach on Lake Superior, great for picking agates.

A BIT OF HISTORY

Iroqouis Point became so named as the result of an epic battle that took place on the spot in 1662. That battle altered the course of history. The entire Whitefish Bay area is the traditional heartland of the "original people", the Anishinabeg. Today we refer to these people as the Chippewa Indians, also known as the Ojibway. In the 1600s, Iroquois from the east were encroaching on this area. There were routes through the region that were important to the fur trade, and therefore, important to the Europeans.

The story goes that a war party of Iroquois had traveled from what is now Western New York state, 400 miles to the east. They were camped near the place where the lighthouse now stands. These Iroquois were a war party, sent to assess the wealth of the area and to take control of the trade routes. The Chippewa spied on the Iroquois, watching their movements and determining their strength. They fell upon the Iroquois one morning at dawn, aided by a dense fog. The Iroquois were caught by surprise and were wiped out. Only two, out of more than 100 were allowed to live. Those two were supplied with a canoe and sent back east with instructions to warn their people to never approach Chippewa territory again.

This battle was no small skirmish, it changed the course of Ojibway history. This was also the first defeat the Iroquois had experienced at the hands of an enemy tribe. In those days, the name of the of the battle was chosen by the victors. The Ojibway chose the name, "Nau-di-we-e-gin-ing", meaning "place of the Iroquois bones". Apparently, the vanquished were not buried. Another story tells of a fur trader, from Sault Ste. Marie, observing human bones and skulls at Iroquois Point in the late 1700s. Few visitors to Iroquois Point are aware of these momentous events from long ago.

AWESOME BEACHES

If you are traveling west, perhaps to Tahquamenon Falls, the Byway becomes Curly Lewis Road out near Naomikong Point. Here are pristine sands on the shore of Lake Superior, surrounded by a national forest. Every time I go through I am amazed at the fact that these beaches are usually empty. If you are looking for a spot to pause and relax on this scenic drive, try these beaches.

SOME

SAY

GOLD

IS

BURIED

NEAR

THE

LANGLEY

BRIDGE

LONGEST COVERED BRIDGE

Our state has only a few original covered bridges remaining. The longest covered bridge in Michigan, is the Langley Bridge, in St. Joseph County. It crosses the St. Joseph River north of Centreville. That stretch of the St. Joseph River has been the site of countless historic events in the Michigan story.

The Langley Bridge extends 282 feet across the river. It has three spans of 94 feet each and is constructed with top quality white pine using the Howe truss system. The bridge was completed in 1887. You won't have any problem identifying the bridge. It is 16 feet high and 19 feet wide. The entire structure is enclosed and is painted a brilliant red. The bridge had to be raised eight feet when the Sturgis Dam was built in 1910, but it still sits very low near the water. One wonders how it survives spring flood waters and ice break up? There is a turn off on the north end that gives an excellent view for photography. It is a pretty good fishing spot too.

There is a story of gold buried nearby. Back in 1838, Isaac Middaugh was on his way north, on the stagecoach route. The stage stopped for the night some way east of here in Branch County. There was talk among the locals about a big dance and hoedown that was to take place in nearby Branch that very evening. Mr. Middaugh decided that a little fun would make for a nice break from the long journey. Now Middaugh happened to be carrying a large quantity of gold coins, and was concerned about road bandits, on the lonely road to the dance hall and back. He took the precaution of waiting until dark and then buried his fortune, on the bank of the nearby St. Joseph River, near the mill keeping just enough on hand for the evening. It is reported that he had a very good time and rumor has it that there was some "special" punch being served behind the dance hall by a couple of local micro-brewers.

Next morning the dancing traveler woke up with a legendary hangover. He didn't have time for breakfast, before the coach was scheduled to depart, because he needed to go out to the the river bank and recover his buried gold. Legend has it, that it didn't work out that way. Search as he would he couldn't find the spot where he had buried his fortune in the dark. He never did. Branch is a ghost town today, but if you can find the foundations of the old mill you might find gold.

M-22 SCENIC DRIVE

One of the most popular scenic drives in Michigan is Route M-22. The most beautiful part of the drive is from Onekema, in the south up to Glen Haven, in the north. Another stretch that is gorgeous is north from Glen Arbor to Northport. This drive is a winding road with several elevation changes and steep hills. Fantastic views of Lake Michigan are visible from several spots along the way. There are a number of convenient spots to pull off the road for a break and picture taking. There are so many of points of interest that this drive can turn into a two or three day tour. Here are a some of the stops running south to north.

A few miles north of Onekema, is a small side road, leading to Pierport. There is an excellent beach on Lake Michigan there. It is maybe the smallest beach on the lake and is popular with locals. Pierport was a lumber town back in the timber era. It was famous for the water. You could build a house and simply shove a pipe into the ground and out would come pure spring water. If you are observant, you will spot one of these old spring fountains still at work. A plaque at the site gives the name as "Old Faceful". North of Pierport is the CMS Nature Preserve with even more breath-taking views. As you reach the top of the hill approaching Elberta, there are a couple of scenic lookouts. When you get out of the car and look to the north, you will see all of Frankfort, nestled in the Betsie Valley, with the sparkling river and harbor spread out below.

The Cabbage Shed in Elberta, on Betsie Bay, is a cool place for lunch. It used to be an actual cabbage warehouse, used to store cabbages waiting for shipment across Lake Michigan. They describe themselves as a "rustic, stalwart spot offering pub grub, scotches & draft beer, plus live music & a lakefront patio". The food is really good, they know how to build a Guinness, and have the best borscht in the north.

Across the bay from Elberta is Frankfort, Michigan. The Frankfort Hotel has a long history and is pretty well known for being haunted fifteen ways to Sunday. A few miles north of Frankfort is the Betsie Point Lighthouse.

Rolling on north brings you to the Sleeping Bear Dunes National Lakeshore. Empire is the first town you reach, and is home to the Empire Bluffs Trail, with its' incredible views of Lake Michigan. This is also the jumping off place for touring Port Oneida.

Extending the drive north will take you to Leland. The "fishing village" with its vintage dock and fish markets is the subject of countless paintings. The northern most tip of M-22 brings you to Northport. The town boasts an historic mill, unbeatable bakery, and great trails.

There is more along Route 22. One of the most popular features of this drive, has been the Route M-22 signs, that mark the road. So many of these iconic signs have vanished, that the State of Michigan is considering changing the sign to simply read 22. It is no small thing, it costs more than $300.00 to replace each sign that disappears, and they keep disappearing.

H-63

FOLLOWS

THE

COURSE

OF

AN

ANCIENT

FOOT

TRAIL

MACKINAC TRAIL DRIVE

When you cross the Straits of Mackinac to the upper peninsula, the first community you come to is St. Ignace. A bit over 50 miles north is Sault Ste. Marie. Most travelers make that drive on I-75, at around 70 miles per hour. If you have a little time, there is a scenic route.

H-63 is a two-lane paved road that runs from St. Ignace to Sault Ste. Marie. At one time, back when the ferry was the only way across the Straits, it was the only road to the "Soo". Even though you are only a few yards from I-75, which runs on a nearly parallel course, if you drive both of these you would swear these roads are in different worlds. The highway is the highway, and you rush along with everyone else, in a hurry to get there. H-63, the old Mackinac Trail, winds along the same course, but is surrounded by evergreen trees and not much else. If you go in the winter, about the only thing you are liable to encounter is a deer or a snowmobile, and gently falling snowflakes.

There are historic towns along the way. Rudyard was chopped out of the forest and bailed out of the swamp. The men who cut the Mackinaw Road through here found sleep impossible due to the clouds of mosquitoes. The only solution was to travel to the Soo at night. Then there is Kinross, site of a famous UFO case. In the 1950s the Air Force operated a radar station here. On November 12, 1953 radar operators are watching empty screens when a blip that shouldn't be there appears over northern Michigan. They scramble an F89 fighter jet to intercept the target and investigate. Traveling at about 500 mph, the fighter closed with the target quickly. When the fighter was around 100 miles from Sault Ste. Marie, the blip from the fighter seemed to merge with the blip from the unknown object. Then the blip faded from the screen and the fighter was never heard from again.

There are high spots at each end of this drive if you want to see the surrounding area. At St. Ignace there is Castle Rock. At Sault Ste. Marie is the Tower of History. Each puts you up 200+ feet for an awesome view. H-63 is found at the second St. Ignace exit.

MAGIC CAPITOL OF THE WORLD

Harry Blackstone became famous for his jaw-dropping magic performances. He was easily the most famous magician of his day, inspiring many a spell-bound youth, to learn the secrets of the magicians. In 1925, Magician Harry Blackstone, moved to Colon, Michigan. He and his brother Pete Bouton, along with the stage crew, would polish their stage show of illusions during the summer months, in preparation for their annual fall and winter tour, throughout the United States. In 1927, Australian magician/ventriloquist Percy Abbott was invited to Colon by Blackstone. The two hit upon the idea of opening a magic manufacturing company - Blackstone Magic Company. However, it was short lived and the partnership lasted only 18 months.

There is still magic in this friendly community in south central Michigan. Downtown has a variety of fun shops and cafe's, and two very professional magic companies. Abbott Magic is on the west end of town. This is one of the oldest magic companies anywhere and they produce great magic tricks today. Fab Magic is on the east end of town and is also reknown manufacturer of magic items. Both of these companies preserve the great traditions, manufacture magic paraphernalia, and they both conduct live performances. In fact, magic is liable to break out anytime you enter one of these shops.

Colon really is the magic capitol of the world. Every year, for more than 75 years, magicians from all over the world have held a gathering here. If you want to join in the fun, all you have to do is show up for the annual festival, Magic Week. There are often more than 1,000 magicians with scheduled performances and impromptu acts of magic possible on any street corner or in any park.

You can easily make a day of it in Colon in most any season. The town and area have a colorful history that is unique in all of Michigan. Just a block north of the main shopping district, is an old church adorned with an enormous clock. When you find this you have found the museum. From the street it appears to be another, rather small church building, that has been converted to a museum. Looks can be an illusion like so many illusions in this community of magic. There is an addition, that more than triples the original size, that is hidden from view from the front. The church and the addition are filled with historical treasures.

Paddlers and fishermen come here for the water

sports. Right on the edge of downtown Colon, are lakes that are known for the fantastic fishing. A dam on the river forms one of the lakes and that one is filled with stumps. All fishermen know what those stumps mean. A block away is an excellent bait and tackle shop.

Then there are the eagles and the hummingbirds. In the past several years there have been Bald Eagles nesting just outside of town. Ask any of the locals which road to take. The eagles have built enormous nests in trees in a farm field. They are usually easy to see from the road. Hummingbird lovers should visit the River Lake Inn on Ralston Road. There are extensive gardens, with walking trails, adjacent to the outdoor dining area. It is not unusual to have hummingbirds visiting the feeders that are right near the tables.

Directions: Colon is in St. Joseph County on Route 86 south of Battle Creek.

MAGICIANS

GATHER

IN COLON

EVERY YEAR

TO

CELEBRATE

MAGIC WEEK

McCOURTIE PARK

In the middle of southern Michigan is a region that has become known as the "Irish Hills". A short and scenic drive from major metropolitan areas, the Irish Hills has been a day trip destination since Henry Ford was building his cars. A cruise along U.S. 12, the Great Sauk Trail, goes right through the hills. The two towers, now closed, were a popular destination back in the day. McCourtie Park however, has only grown in popularity as a day trip destination. Almost directly south of Jackson on U.S. 12 is Somerset Township. Just east of Somerset Center a small sign announces McCourtie Park.

The Park is several acres in size, containing a number of very unique features, along with beautiful grounds and a meandering stream. On nice summer and autumn days, it is a favorite destination for a picnic, a tranquil walk along the trails, or fun and games with the puppy dog. Upon entering the park visitors find unique works of art scattered along the paved path. A small stream meanders through the park. That stream can be crossed on any one of 17 bridges. Each bridge is of a different design. One looks like a log bridge, another like a suspension bridge, and another like a thatch roofed bridge. Seventeen in all; all different; all the work of one artist, and all are constructed of concrete. McCourtie Park is a favorite spot for bird watchers as well. On top of tall poles, are two of the largest Purple Martin bird houses, anywhere in the mid-west. Beautifully constructed with sculptured roofs, each is said to house more than 100 Purple Martins.

There is more to discover in this park, and some of it is underground. If you bear to the left, as you enter the park on the paved path, you go up a small grassy hill. There is an historic marker there with some interesting information and there are two tall tree trunks with broken branches that are an unnatural white color. The color is due to the fact, that these two trees are also constructed of concrete and are actually chimneys that served an underground rathskeller that once operated here. If you go back to the paved path and walk along you will come to the fronting of that grassy hill. Installed in the face of the hill are what appear to be old garage doors. Last visit, one could peer inside through one or two windows, and see the rathskeller is still there. A beautiful mahogany bar, fixtures, and a floor to ceiling field stone fireplace are all still there.

MIRROR OF HEAVEN

Kitch-iti-kipi (cold big water) is the largest spring in Michigan at 300 feet by 175 feet. Fed by more than 20 springs, it is refreshed continuously with crystal-clear water. More than 10,000 gallons a minute gush up from the limestone bed. Also known as "The Big Spring", Kitch-iti-kipi can be visited all year long. The water remains at a steady 45 degrees, so it rarely freezes in winter. During the warm seasons visitors can travel across the spring on a raft. The raft can be self-operated and is equipped with viewing windows. The water is crystal-clear affording a good view of the log strewn floor of the spring and the huge trout that live there.

There are several legends associated with the 40+ foot deep pool. One is that in the past, some of the springs would spout columns of water high into the air. Imagine happening onto an unfrozen body of water in the dead of winter. Obviously, this cold water would be thought to have magical qualities.

Another legend may explain the pattern at the bottom of the spring, that some say resembles a beautiful native American maiden. While her lover was absent she was trying to elude an unwanted suitor and dove into the spring. The magical qualities of the waters transformed her into a white deer. From this event came the taboo among native tribes against the killing of white deer. There are other legends including the idea that the waters were lethal since they don't freeze in winter and no frogs or turtles live in the pool.

A Little History: John I. Bellaire, a Manistique businessman, stumbled onto the spring in the early 1900's. He was captivated by the crystal-clear pool and decided to take action to preserve the spring. He could have bought the property for himself, but he wanted the spring preserved for all to enjoy. In 1926 he contacted the Palms Book Land Company and facilitated the purchase of almost 90 acres of land by the State of Michigan for $10. The deed requires the property "to be forever used as a public park, bearing the name Palms Book State Park." Additional land has been acquired by the State of Michigan, so the park now encompasses 308 acres, so the dreams and legends live on. While at the park, you can enjoy a picnic and take advantage of the facilities for a nice rest. There is plenty of parking, and it is an easy walk to the spring along a paved path. There is a State Park fee.

Directions: The "Big Spring", Kitch-iti-kipi, is located just west of Manistique, at Palms Book

State Park, at the end of M-149. From downtown Manistique, go across the river, where the old siphon bridge is, and follow the signs, or go west from Manistique on US 2 to Thompson, take M-149 north for 12 miles to the park.

THE

MISTAKE

ON

THE

LAKE

CREATED

THE

BEAUTIFUL

BEULAH

BEACH

MISTAKE ON THE LAKE

Michigan has several lakes named, Crystal Lake. In the case of the one at Beulah, the name is an accurate description. The watershed that feeds Crystal Lake is very small and fertilizer and silt outflows are minimal, leading to the exceptionally clear water. This is also the largest lake in Michigan with that name. Crystal Lake measures approximately 2.5 by 8 miles and has a maximum depth of 165 feet. At 9,854 acres, it is Michigan's ninth largest inland lake. Today the lake is surrounded by beautiful sandy beaches and is a popular summer destination. Things weren't always that way.

Up to and through the American Civil War years, Crystal Lake was known as "Cap Lake". That name was due to the frequent whitecaps visible on its surface. The surrounding area was heavily forested with steep hills. Then in 1873, Archibald Jones had an idea. He wanted to improve his shipping business. He decided to open a channel, to connect Crystal Lake to Lake Michigan, just a few miles away. This would greatly facilitate the movement of commodities to the Great Lakes shipping ports.

The mistake Mr. Jones made has even been called the "Tragedy of Crystal Lake", was that he failed to recognize the differences in water levels of the two bodies of water. The lake level of Crystal Lake was higher than the level of Lake Michigan. The channel was dug according to plan. When the Crystal lake end was opened, the lake water poured into the channel, and the water level in Crystal Lake dropped. Although the project was a failure, the lowering of the lake level uncovered sandy beaches including the current public beach at Beulah.

They like to have fun in northern Michigan and festivals are fun. In Beulah, they celebrate "Archibald Jones Day" at the Village Park every year. Activities for all ages include a walking tour of Beulah, and the waterfront area, as well as a wide variety of "Victorian era" games. There is a simulation of the lowering of the lake, as well as hearing Mr. Jones tell his side of the story. Following Mr. Jones speech there is a sing-along and a birthday celebration, in honor of his birthday.

Directions: Crystal Lake, Downtown Beulah, and the beach, are on Route 31, south of the Sleeping Bear Dunes.

OCQUEOC FALLS

Ocqueoc Falls is the largest waterfall in the lower peninsula of Michigan. The word "ocqueoc" comes from the French for "crooked waters". The name fits. The Ocqueoc River does in fact wind all over in its course across the karst formations in Presque Isle county. Size is only one of the unique features of this waterfall. One of its best features is that it is easy to get to. In fact, this may be the only universally accessible waterfall in the United States. The parking lot is only a few yards from the falls. This is not a big plunge falls, like many in the upper peninsula, it is more an extended cascade with the longest of three drops being only about 5 feet or so. The gentle angle of the falls and its proximity to the picnic area make this a popular wilderness swimming spot.

There is another unusual feature about this area that adds to the fun of a trip to Ocqueoc. The entire region sits atop a limestone formation known as a karst. As the river flows across the limestone, it cuts channels into the river bed. Several branches of this river, especially the Little Ocqueoc, have parts of their course running underground. You can walk along a nearby two track and, suddenly, there is the river flowing right out of the side of a hill. During spawning season, you can see the salmon actually swim through these underground channels. The Ocqueoc River is one of the few rivers in the Lower Peninsula to flow north.

Upon arrival, some visitors head right to the falls. Others stop and visit with the kid in the hot dog costume for a quick snack. Another option at Ocqueoc Falls is to take a hike along the Ocqueoc Bicentennial Pathway. The pathway has groomed winter trails and summer hiking trails. There are several loops. The first is the shortest and, some say, most scenic. The remnants of an old mill race can be seen just above the falls. The trail takes visitors through a beautiful area of the river valley that is forested by towering pines and hardwoods. The trail is usually in good shape and is shared with mountain bikers.

When I first heard about the underground river, I pictured a great mystical cavern. I imagined wandering through stalagmites and stalactites with a torch, sputtering in the darkness. I spent a couple hours stumbling around the forest trying to find a cave entrance to the "great underground river". Finally, a kindly local took pity and explained it all to me. No, there isn't a mystical cavern to explore. However, there are places where the river disappears underground and reappears on the surface some distance away. On a quiet day, you can hear the river flowing underground in some places. One spot, that is easy to reach, where the water bubbles out of the hillside is on the Silver River nearby.

As mentioned, a youngster in a hot dog costume may be selling hot dogs at the falls during the warm months. For winter visitors, the nearby Purple Store is ready to serve up warm drinks and delicious baked goods. The actual name of the store is M-211 Mercantile Market, but everybody calls it the Purple Store. They also have a large chalkboard map of the area showing the falls, underground river and other local attractions.

Directions: The day-use area for Ocqueoc Falls is on Ocqueoc Falls Road, which can be reached from Rogers City by following M-68 west for a bit over 11 miles.

The Purple Store is on M-211 a few miles north of Onaway.

DRUMMOND

ISLAND

IS

EAST

OF

THE

UPPER

PENINSULA

OFF THE GRID GETAWAY

We hear about getaways to remote destinations where the experience includes being off the grid. These trips can be far away, expensive and can involve real inconvenience for those who aren't familiar with life in the wild. In many cases off the grid means you will be roughing it. Steep cliffs to climb, glaciers to negotiate, bug infested tropical rain forests and just plain general discomfort. I know, the challenges are supposed to be part of the experience, but there is an alternative. Drummond Island Adventures with Captain Jennifer Starr make it convenient anyone can experience the solitude and beauty of an off-grid getaway. Describing these excursions Jen says, "Please come and visit me, let me show you some of the wonders of living off grid, on a beautiful island, rich with history, where nature abounds and lifts your soul!"

The "Off the Grid" adventure has several components, each chosen to reveal the natural beauty and rich history of Drummond Island. Across a few days you will experience the island from land, sea and air. One day is a kayak tour of Scammon Cove. While loons call in the distance and eagles soar in the sky above, you paddle around the cove. The sunken tug "Silver Spray" is right below the waves. At another point the ruins of the lumber dock and mill are the highlight. Then on to the Wayfarer's Mart and the Stone house, the only structures remaining of the town of Johnswood.

Another day will be a chartered fishing trip. Drummond is known for great fishing and, depending on the season, anglers can expect to catch perch, trout and salmon. It can be windy out on the lake, so plan to have warm clothing as well as your sunglasses and camera. The next day may include a late afternoon sea plane tour of the island, ending in a water landing at a private campsite. At the campsite everything will be set up for an evening on the lakeshore gazing at those incredible night skies. The following morning the sea plane returns to transport the campers back to Jen's Den for a bit more kayaking and personal time touring the island.

Every detail required for a successful adventure is attended to by Captain Jennifer Starr, acting as host and private tour guide. Along the way she shares stories, legends and real history of the places on the tour. The colorful history of Scammon Cove, the Island Cedar Company, the lore of the Finnish community and the rise and fall of the town of Johnswood are just some of the tales that will be told.

This Drummond Island property is 34 acres on Scammon Cove with the ruins of the old mill visible in the distance. Jen's Den is a mix of rustic and industrial design. A pole barn, with living quarters above, provides modern off-grid accommodations. The grounds include acres of pristine forest and 1,000 feet of waterfront. The adventures are geared toward single travelers or couples, so you get a lot of personal attention. The facilities are not designed to accommodate large groups. Adventure opportunities are limited in number. Full details about these off the grid adventures can be found at www.jensdenoffgrid. com

THERE

ARE

PREHISTORIC

MINES

ALL

AROUND

OLD

VICTORIA

OLD VICTORIA – SCENIC DRIVE

About 18 miles south and east out of Ontonagon is a site that was an early attempt at copper mining by Europeans in Michigan. Originally known as Finn Town, Old Victoria was established more than a hundred years ago. Judging by the size of the development it was a very serious effort.

A tour of the area includes log structures that have been restored by the historical society. Several of the cabins can be viewed from the road, but taking the tour gets you up close and inside. Getting a good look at the dove-tail construction of these hand-hewn cabins gives one a new appreciation for the ingenuity of these miners. The furnishings and old pot belly stoves add to the experience of stepping back in time. Spending a winter in one of these cabins, and the necessary trip to the out house, must have required real toughness.

In Rockland there are a couple of unique businesses. The Rockland Depot is a general store. Be sure to ask to see the Spice Vault. They have rare and unusual spices from all over the world. Henry's Never Inn remains a favorite destination. It sports a stunning mahogany bar and they produce one of the best Pasty's in the upper peninsula from a recipe that has been in the family for four generations.

Directions: Old Victoria is west of Rockland. Rockland is on Route 45 about 12 miles south of Ontonagon. Watch carefully for the small sign in town pointing the way. The historical museum is in Rockland. The staff can give directions to the old ghost town.

OSPREY ROOST

Fletcher Pond is a wonderful and wild place for outdoor fun. Montmorency County, east of Gaylord, contains one of the most remarkable bodies of water in Michigan, and this is in a state known as a water wonderland. Also known as the Fletcher Flooding, this body of water has something for everyone except sandy beaches. Fletcher Pond is an impoundment, created by the construction of a dam, on one branch of the Thunder Bay River. A 9,000 acre shallow water paradise is the result. This is the perfect destination for bird watchers, fishermen and nature enthusiasts. There are no vast sandy beaches and about the only spot where you can fish from shore is the public launch on Fletcher Landing Road.

This is a relatively unspoiled area, with little development on the water, and just a few lodging establishments on the shore itself. The water is shallow and full of stumps, trees and even part of a sunken railroad. The result is a perfect environment for fish to thrive. Six pound bass are here and the northern pike regularly exceed 30 inches. The heavy cover in the water and the stumps also make the pond unpopular for jet skis or large power boats, though power fishing boats are used along the river bed. Consequently, this is one of the quietest places in Michigan to fish, canoe or kayak.

Osprey abound here. In fact, this is one of the largest populations of osprey east of the Mississippi River. There are more than 20 osprey nesting platforms. The best way to observe them is from a boat with binoculars. There is nothing quite like seeing an osprey come exploding up out of the lake after it dives after a fish. It is really awesome unless that was the fish you were after. The bird watchers love this place. In addition to the osprey, there are egrets, geese, all kinds of ducks, and herons.

Along the way, you may spot an elk. Just a few miles to the west is Michigan Elk Country. An easy drive is Route 459, out of Hillman, going west and picking up Route 624. Keep going west and you will hit Route 33. Go south to Atlanta, the Elk Capital of Michigan. Elk are best viewed at dawn and dusk in the open fields. The local guides know the best spots.

The nearest town is Hillman, Michigan, on Route 32 between Gaylord and Alpena. The Fletcher Flooding is south of Hillman, and can be reached from Jacks Landing Rd. or take Farrier Rd. south to Conners Landing Rd.

PIGS FIND A FORTUNE

Up on the Keweenaw Peninsula, copper country legends abound about fortunes found and lost. Some say that the famous Calumet Conglomerate was discovered, or rediscovered because some pigs made a break for the wide open spaces.

Back in the 1800s, Ed Hulbert ran a boarding house called the Half Way House. One night it seems that some folks came asking for help. They were trying to find some runaway pigs. The story goes that the pigs evaded the searchers that night, but the search began again the next morning. One group of searchers heard pigs snuffling around and the sound seemed to come from under ground. After scouring the crags and underbrush, a large pit was found. Sure enough, there were the pigs rooting around, happy as pigs in a mud hole.

That pit contained rubble, tailings, and prehistoric stone tools. A further search eventually led to the discovery of the Calumet Conglomerate, a copper lode that was 35 miles long. A mining company was established which became the Calumet and Hecla. Millions of pounds of copper were recovered, and Calumet grew into one of the jewels of the Keweenaw Peninsula.

A visit to Calumet should be on every itinerary that takes you to the western upper peninsula. The entire downtown is a National Historic Landmark District. St. Ann's Church is one of the most beautiful in copper country. The Calumet Theatre is a National Historic Landmark and, in my opinion, is one of the two most beautiful theatres in Michigan. A tour of the Coppertown Mining Museum provides excellent information about the unique history of this region.

A favorite side trip, out of Calumet, is the short drive to Cliff. About 14 miles further north from Calumet is the town of Phoenix. 3 or 4 miles before you get there, is a small sign by the side of the road. It simply reads "Cliff Cemetery". If it is safe to do so, pull off, and follow the old path into the forest. After a short walk, you will be in the old cemetery that served the town of Clifton. After your visit, continue north and you will find the old ghost town, now a museum complex.

While not discovered by pigs, this was the Keweenaw's first profitable mine, eventually producing 40 million pounds of copper. This is rough country. Tough people came here and wrested a living from the rocks. Their story is told by the stones in the cemetery at the bottom of the cliff.

POINT ABBAYE'

This is one of the most beautiful spots in
Michigan that most casual travelers have never
heard of. It is also a rather remote spot and will
require investing the better part of a full day to
visit. At Point Abbaye' the waves of Lake
Superior pound and crash on the wind-swept
rocks. The Huron Mountains are on the horizon.
At this unspoiled place, you can almost hear the
rigging of the tall ships of French explorers, as
they entered this magical region 400 years ago. If
you look to your left, you can see the iron range
of the Keweenaw Peninsula, and to your right,
you can see the wilds of the Huron Mountains.
This is one of the few places in Michigan where
both are visible.

Point Abbaye' is at the very end of a small
peninsula that juts out into Lake Superior between
Keweenaw Bay and Huron Bay. The trip involves
an eleven-mile drive on an old sandy two track, or
"snake trail", as we used to call them. This track
is ROUGH, and your top speed will be about 15
miles per hour. You cruise through the wilderness
past a few isolated homes, and through the
silence, broken only by bird calls and the music of
Lake Superior. At the end of this drive, you will
enter a small parking area that is not paved. There

are rustic outhouses. It is entirely possible that you will be the only one there.

There are two or three hiking trails marked out that lead to the point itself. The trails are also unimproved and a little rough, but they will get you there. Other than drinking water and a camera, no special equipment is required. The shortest trail will get you out to Point Abbaye' in 15 or 20 minutes. When you get there, you leave the forest and step out onto an enormous rock shelf that overlooks the lake. Care should be taken as the rocks can be slippery and there are no facilities here, this is pure Michigan wilderness. The view of the lake, the distant Huron Islands, and the mountains makes it all worth it.

When you decide you have had enough natural beauty and want to return to your car, there is an option other than taking the trails back. The physically fit and adventurous might want to walk back along the shoreline. The entire way is nothing but rocks and rock cliffs with huge splashes of spray, great giant pines and the cold waters of Lake Superior forming pools and rivulets. If you keep Lake Superior on your right hand side you will eventually get back to the parking area. The hike along the shore is extremely rough, slippery, and can be wet if the wind is up. However, it is just too beautiful, and you can get pictures like no other.

Directions: First we have to get to Aura, home of the Aura Music Jamboree. The easiest way is to take the Pequaming road out of L'Anse. L'Anse is at the southern tip of Keweenaw Bay between Negaunee and Ontonagon. After you pass the small settlement of Pequaming, you will continue until you reach the even smaller settlement of Aura, Michigan. At the crossroads, in Aura, turn north and continue until the pavement ends, it is less than a half mile. Where the pavement ends is where you find the two track trail leading into the forest. This two track is extremely rough. If you take that trail about eleven miles, you will come to Point Abbaye'. The only other way to get there is by water. This is not a trip recommended for winter, unless you know what you are doing with a snow machine.

AURA

IS HOME

TO A

FINNISH

FOLK

MUSIC

FESTIVAL

PORT ONEIDA

Port Oneida is one of the most unique historic districts in all of Michigan. Located within the borders of the Sleeping Bear National Lakeshore, it is one of the least visited attractions in the entire area. Perhaps that is because it doesn't appear on all Michigan maps. Empire is shown, as is Pyramid Point, but not Port Oneida.

Port Oneida grew into a sizable community in the late 1800's as a result of the lumber industry and the work of Thomas Kelderhouse. Eventually the area included a dock on Lake Michigan, blacksmith shop, post office, general store, and a boarding house. When the trees were gone the dock and mill were closed. By 1908 all of the buildings of the original town site, except the Kelderhouse residence, had been abandoned. A number of small farms struggled for existence. Most were no longer farmed after World War II.

When you enter the park at Empire, make a quick stop at the ranger station to pick up the Port Oneida booklet. It has descriptions of the buildings and a simple map. You'll need the map to find you way around the district. The trip through the Port Oneida Historic District can be enjoyed by car or bicycle. Note that some of these farms are on gravel roads. The tour meanders through the agricultural area of Pyramid Point and takes you to 10 - 15 farmsteads, and the old Port Oneida schoolhouse. The Bay View Hiking Trail also runs through the district and offers a convenient way to see some of the more remote parts of the district.

The Charles Olsen Farm is one of the first stops you will come to. The Preserve Historic Sleeping Bear office is located at this farm, and if open, is a good source for additional information. While you go from farm to farm, you will also come across the Kelderhouse Cemetery and the farm next to it. The present house has also been used as a grocery store, telephone exchange and post office. Some of the barns are worth visiting like the Miller Barn. There is old machinery scattered around and some of the barns still have huge field stones as part of their foundations.

Most of the buildings are well preserved and visitors are encouraged to wander around. Some, like the Weaver Farm, are badly weathered and in poor condition. It is not unusual to spend a couple of hours here and only see one or two other people. You can really enjoy the quiet and isolation of these beautiful farm lands.

One of the most photographed barns in Michigan is on the nearby D. H. Day farmstead. The barn, built in the late 1800's, has twin silos and an ogee (bell-shaped) roof with octagonal cupolas topping it all off. You really can't miss it. It doesn't lie in the district but is within the boundaries of the park.

Directions: From Frankfort go north on M-22 through Empire and into the park. From Traverse City go west on M-72 until you reach the park entrance at Empire.

SLEEPING

BEAR DUNES

GOT THE

NAME

FROM

NATIVE AMERICAN

ORAL

HISTORIES

RIDE THE BREEZEWAY

The "Breezeway" is a designated scenic drive, east and west, across southern Charlevoix County. The ride is about 25 miles from Atwood on the west end to Boyne Falls on the east end. In the middle is East Jordan, at the southern extreme of Lake Charlevoix. Most of the Breezeway follows route C-48. This scenic drive proves the saying that the journey is the point, not how fast you can get from place to place. The BREEZEWAY is as cool a ride as you will find in any part of Michigan. This is drumlin country (drumlins are rare glacial hill formations), so the road is hilly as it winds through beautiful country.

The ride can take a while if you stop at the numerous attractions along the way. There are u-pick farms, soap makers, Raven Hill Discovery Center, Central Lakes Iron Works, The Blue Pelican Inn, and the very cool Ironton Ferry among others. There is enough to see on this back road ride that some folks go from west to east, turn around, and go back the other way. The drumlin formations create long straight hills running north and south. During color tour time, the vistas from the tops of some of the hills are breathtaking.

The road is a two lane paved county road. Along

the route are broad fields, colorful hardwood forests, and wetlands. In East Jordan, about in the middle of the Breezeway, is a large wetland. Nearly any time of year there will be swans nesting there.

ROAD TO HELL

There actually is a road to hell, it leads to Hell, Michigan and it is paved. The road to Hell is named D-32. This great ride takes you through hills and around curves, over rivers and along lakes. In many places the trees arch completely over the road. The motorcycle riders have known about this for a while, but unless you are going to Hell, you may have missed it. Taking this scenic drive is a pleasant and easy way to enjoy an afternoon trip. While the drive is only a few miles, the surrounding region is full of places to discover.

The road you are looking for is D-32. It runs from Gregory to Pinckney with Hell in the middle, winding through the trees next to the Edwin S. George Reserve. Along the way you will find Gosling Lake, Half Moon Lake and Brum Lake among a half dozen others. When you arrive in Hell you will find a couple of small shops and places for a meal. In past visits the General Store acted as the Post Office. If you remember, bring something to mail so it will have a Hell, Michigan post mark. At one time, the Post Office would singe the corner of your envelope.

If you like outdoor activities, you might take some

equipment with you. In town you can rent kayaks and canoes. Within a couple of miles are a number of hiking trail complexes, multiple lakes and streams and a number of parks that have both water and picnic areas. No doubt you have heard of a marriage going to hell in a hand basket. Well, with a little planning you can start out on the road of marital bliss by getting married in Hell. They do have a chapel and couples do get married there all the time. At the last visit, you could still buy your own small patch of Hell for $6.66.

Directions: The road to Hell is in south central Michigan about mid-way between Lansing and Ann Arbor. Take Route 52 north from I-94 or south from I-96 then take 106 east toward Unadilla. You can also take U.S.23 and get the Pinckney Road between Ann Arbor and Brighton.

SAILORS PINES

At Sailors Pines you can still take a walk through an old growth forest in the lower peninsula. The last wave of the lumber era was passing in the 1920's in mid-Michigan. At the same time, Mr. William Sailors began to review his timberland holdings in Newaygo County. He discovered that he had several acres of white pine that were maturing but were not yet large enough for harvesting. He had participated in the lumber boom and had seen the fantastic giant pines toppled forest by forest. After that, the hardwoods were harvested, and the land was cleared of the wondrous old trees. But not all of it. While dealing in hardwoods, Mr. Sailors discovered a neglected stand of white pines and decided to preserve them. His son, David, carried on this work and the result is a stand of virgin pines, a quiet place available to everyone. James Sailors is the current owner and the pines have matured to a point similar to what lumberjacks would have found in the 1800s.

You can pull into the trees and park. You can walk just a few yards in and will be surrounded by enormous old Michigan white pine trees. Many are more than 30" in diameter and several are more than 100' tall. Wander along the path for a bit longer and feel yourself transported to a quieter time and a less-hurried pace. If you bring a picnic lunch, you can pause long enough for your inner self to slow down and become quiet enough to hear the winds whispering in the pines, hear deer walking nearby and glimpse wild turkeys foraging. All of this is just a few minutes from town and easily accessible by car. The road going to the pines is even paved. Sailors Pines are easy to get to at any time of day, but the solitude is truly amazing at sunrise.

You are welcome here and can bring a lunch; however, no camping is allowed and NO FIRES.

Directions: The short version is that the pines are located at 52nd Street, 1/4 mile east of Locust Ave. From Newaygo, go north across the river and go east on Croton Dr. Just before you reach the dam turn north on Pear Ave. After a couple of miles, you will hit 52nd Street. Go right, jog left and then right again and you will find the Pines.

SANDHILL CRANE FESTIVAL

Every October Sandhill Cranes gather by the thousands in southwest Michigan. This is said to be the second largest gathering of these birds in the U.S. They come flying and soaring into the wetlands in the Baker Sanctuary, the air filled with that distinctive, almost prehistoric cry. For more than 15 years the Michigan Audubon Society and the Kiwanis Club have opened the Kiwanis Youth Area to the public for the Sandhill Crane Festival on the second weekend in October.

The area where the festival is held is rather wild and the road in and parking areas are not paved. The festival is spread around a central building where educational programs and materials are available. There are usually arts and crafts that are on theme created by some very talented artists. There is an interactive program featuring live raptors. These birds of prey are shown on the hillside by local experts.

There are guided walks along the nature trails with expert naturalists, programs about birding and lots of nature exhibits. In past years there have been a number of exotic animals included. A favorite is a desert tortoise. He is a sandy color and charges around the exhibit area, great fun. There are also a couple of short nature trails. One leads into the forest and the other takes you to a crane viewing area.

There are sandhill cranes and lots of them. Past gatherings have been estimated at 4,000+. There are a number of viewing places prepared. About 4:30 pm, the cranes begin to fly in. Huge flocks can be seen gliding down to the wetlands with peak activity after 6 pm. You want to bring a camera and binoculars. A light folding chair comes in handy. This is a nature area and a wetland, choose practical footwear, there are some damp areas.

Directions: Baker Sanctuary is north of Battle Creek. The entrance to the Youth Area is actually off 15 Mile Road. Take Route 78 from Route 66 or from I-69 and keep your eye peeled for signs in the shape of a Sandhill Crane.

THUNDER BAY

A visit to the Great Lakes Maritime Heritage Center will open up a whole new world of discovery. This is the only National Oceanographic and Atmospheric Agency, NOAA, location at a freshwater facility in the world. The facility offers a number of entertaining and educational programs that highlight the value of our irreplaceable natural resources. The conservation and preservation of the Great Lakes, containing 20% of the fresh water on earth, is what the work here is all about.

The Heritage Center is the starting point for exploring the Thunder Bay National Marine Sanctuary that protects the shipwrecks and the diving areas. The welcome center offers 10,000 square feet of interactive exhibits showcasing the history, shipwrecks and archaeology of Thunder Bay specifically, and the Great Lakes in general. There are several excellent maps showing the location of shipwrecks with details about some of the more famous. One unusual exhibit is a full size replica of a wooden Great Lakes schooner. Visitors can climb aboard and experience what a Great Lakes storm would feel like on the tossing deck.

A popular way to explore some of the 100+ shipwrecks, in and near the bay, is by boat. In the warm months, glass bottom boat tours around the bay are available. Which of the wrecks the tour covers depends on wind conditions. Some of the wrecks are more than 80 feet below the surface. Still, they are perfectly visible due to the clarity of these waters. A few miles away is the 40 Mile Point Lighthouse. The Joseph S. Fay became stranded there in 1905. The wreck is still there, in shallow water, making it a favorite to visit.

Among the valuable educational programs supported by the Sanctuary is an underwater robotics competition. The competition allows students to engage in underwater missions using underwater remote operated vehicles. The missions are based on real world scenarios like exploring sunken ships. It was this kind of vehicle that was used to help map and photograph the constructions, deep underwater, on the Alpena-Amberly ridge.

There, on the floor of Lake Huron, is the ancient land bridge that stretched from Alpena to Ontario, 9,000 years ago. The Alpena-Amberly land bridge was a migration route for caribou. Human hunters constructed stone structures designed to channel the animals into killing zones. The structures are still there, deep underwater. When these structures were built, the environment was far different than today. The land bridge was above the water. The immense glacier that was carving out the Great Lakes was receding north. At that time the glacier was only about 100 miles north, and was visible, as it was still nearly a mile thick. Remarkably, the constructions bear a resemblance to those built and in use today in arctic regions, where caribou still follow the annual migration patterns. Without preservation and exploration in clean clear waters, these artifacts might have been lost forever.

TWO

RARE

VARIETIES

OF

TOAD

TRILLIUM

GROW

IN

THE

TRILLIUM

RAVINE

TRILLIUM RAVINE

Southwest Michigan is famous for blueberries, wineries, rivers, and mills. There are also nature areas and botanical gardens scattered across this region. One of the least known is the Trillium Ravine. This wildflower wonderland is in a populated area and is easily accessible. Yet it is so little known that even the locals are often unaware that it exists.

The Trillium Ravine is a Michigan Nature Association project. The preserve covers 14+ acres of mature hardwoods including sugar maples, basswood, ironwood, and red oak, as well as mature beech trees. The ravine itself is roughly 150 yards long, 40 yards wide, and 20 to 30 feet deep. A narrow unimproved trail, less than a mile long, winds along the edge of the ravine and through the woods. At the right time of year, the entire floor of the forest and the ravine itself will be a riot of wildflowers so thick you can hardly leave the path without trampling them. There are the common trilliums in white and pink, thousands of them. There are May apples, trout lilies, and carpets of blue violets. There are rare wildflowers as well. The ravine is home to two species of toad trillium at the northern limit of their range. Also growing here are the prairie trillium and a species of wood poppy that only occurs in Michigan's southwestern counties. For a short time each year this is one of the most beautiful spots in all of southern Michigan.

NOTE: This is a wild place, and the sides of the ravine can be slippery. There is no formal parking lot. The reserve is surrounded by private property. Please respect the boundaries and take out what you take in. Trilliums only bloom for a short time in this location, often peaking around Mother's Day.

Directions: Walton Road runs from Buchanan north and east toward Niles and is exit 7 off U.S. 31. Just east of the interstate take East Geyer Rd. This road winds through a large housing development. After a couple curves and a sharp curve to the right you find yourself on Riverside Road. Stay on Riverside as it curves downhill. Cross the ravine and watch for the Michigan Nature Association sign on the right.

TUNNEL OF TREES

Highway M-119 runs from Harbor Springs to Cross Village in the far northwest of the lower peninsula of Michigan. The road contains 137 curves as it winds along Lake Michigan and is known as the Tunnel of Trees. Some of these spots have a long history like the Old Council Tree and the Devils Elbow. This winding two lane road is a stunningly beautiful drive in all seasons. It is a particular favorite during summer and autumn. Since the whole thing is only about 20 miles it is a favorite day trip. There are some interpretive signs on the drive, explaining the bent trees and other points of interest.

The Tunnel of Trees is home to two unique family businesses. One is the famous Legs Inn in Cross Village known for beautiful gardens and Polish cuisine. The other is the Good Hart General Store in Good Hart. They are famous for their pot pies. On the north edge of Good Hart a small sign pointing to the St. Ignatius Church. Originally established in 1741, the restored church is open for tours and includes a Native American burial ground. South of Good Hart is the Thorne Swift Nature Preserve. There is only a small sign to let you know this 30 acre natural wonderland is there. Three trails totaling 1 ¼ miles are well maintained and offer a nice stroll through the woodlands or down to a smooth stone-filled shore on Lake Michigan. The trails are comfortable and include boardwalks where necessary.

Directions: From the Mackinac Bridge head south to Route 66 and go west to Cross Village. Take M-119 south about 20 miles where the drive ends at Harbor Springs.

TWO TOWERS

Travelers heading west from Detroit, or east from Chicago, still enjoy the "Great Sauk Trail", U.S. 12, and the beautiful scenery of the Irish Hills. East of Route 50 on U.S. 12, stand two nearly identical towers, side by side. The towers have a unique place, in the history of Michigan tourism, and the Irish Hills.

In the early 1900's, the Irish Hills were a local secret, but Michigan tourism was about to change that. At that time, Cambridge Junction, was about as far as you could get on a day trip, out of Detroit, and still make it back home before dark. Getting back early was important. The roads were sketchy, cars had no headlights, and the area was still a wilderness in some ways.

Edward Kelly owned land along the road, and the Michigan Observation Company wanted to buy a bit of it, with the intention of building a viewing tower. Mr. Kelly declined, but his neighbor, Edward Brighton, agreed, and a 50-foot high tower was built on a high spot, and opened in October of 1924. Just in time for folks to travel out, pay five cents, climb to the top, and gaze out at the spectacular fall colors and brilliant blue lakes, scattered through the hills.

The new tower was just six feet from the property line, and Mr. Kelly was miffed. The observation tower obscured the view from his house. To get even, he built a nearly identical tower, just 12 feet from the original. What's more, he made his tower taller than the original, and the feud was on. The Michigan Observation Company raised their observation platform, so it was equal in height to Kelly's "Spite Tower". Further, they let Mr. Kelly know, that if this didn't put an end to the "feud", they would tear their tower down, and build an enormous steel structure, that would dwarf Kelly's. That ended the feud and for several years, the competition was in finding unusual ways to attract visitors, even to the point of bringing in alligators and monkeys.

The two towers were a very successful attraction for more than five decades. At one time, as many as 50 buses per day were bringing tourists, to enjoy the view. The site was open 24 hours per day and offered, in addition to the zoo, a campground, carnival rides, a dance hall, three gas stations, and a miniature golf course. Lodging was available nearby, and three restaurants served travelers. The advent of the automobile brought more visitors, but also spelled doom for the towers. People could travel further, faster and cheaper, and headed for more impressive destinations. By the mid-1960s more than 2 million people had visited the towers. As time passed, various problems plagued a series of owners, and by the mid-1980s the towers shut down.

In 2016, renovations and repairs were underway, to save the towers from demolition. At this writing, the renovation work has stalled.

IT

IS

ALWAYS

1932

AT

THE

WELLINGTON

FARM

WELLINGTON FARM USA

At one time, Wellington Farm was an actual community in northern Michigan. In that era, between the 1880s and the early 1900s, farming had replaced lumbering as the main activity. In 1918 the Wellington Farm post office was closed. After that, those services were provided by the post office in Grayling. With the loss of postal services, businesses and people began to move away. Eventually all that remained were a few scattered buildings.

A few years ago, one man began creating a living history farm, now called Wellington Farm USA. He collected farm equipment, authentic buildings, and stories and histories, from around the region. He built Wellington Farm Park into the living museum. It is located south of Grayling near the site of one of the old post offices.

Wellington Farm USA Park is described as a 60-acre, open-air, interpretive museum. The park gives visitors a chance to experience life as it was in rural America. Everything is as it would have been in 1932, during the Great Depression. There are several restored buildings, including a Blacksmith Shop, Grist Mill, Sawmill, Carpenter's Shop, Machine Shed, Farmer's Market, and Summer Kitchen. The old barnyard serves as a petting zoo. All the shops are functional with restored and authentic equipment inside. During the season, based on availability, craftsmen are in these shops, doing the work in the same way and with the same tools as in the 1930s. Everything is arranged so the visitor can experience living history up close.

The General store is a big favorite, offering produce grown locally. Along side are a variety of flours and grains, produced at the Grist Mill. There are jams, jellies, sauces, and cookbooks. The old Farm Market Building renovation created a Museum of Agriculture, it has a schedule of changing exhibits. The Carpenter's Shop contains rare woodworking tools used to build structures in the nations capitol.

A real jewel on the site is the Stittsville Church. Stittsville, Michigan, originally named Norwich, had a brief life during the timber era. After 1904 the railroad shut down. Then services and businesses began to close as the lumbermen followed the trees north. By 1917, the population was down to 40. Soon everything was gone except the old church and cemetery. The Stittsville Church was nearly forgotten, and would have been lost, but for the efforts of the folks at Wellington Farm Park. In 2005 they acquired the old church, moved it to the park, and began restoration. Complete with bell tower and bell, the church again stands as it did when it was first dedicated in the 1880s.

Another cool feature of Wellington Farm USA is the system of nature trails. The park is spread out across 60 acres. Trails connect the various buildings. Nature trail loops branch off through the beech/maple forest and across the meadows. There are wildflowers along the paths and the forest floor is covered with a variety of ferns. The meadows and fields are where you find Buttercup, Devil's Paintbrush, Indian Paintbrush, and others. In spring the birds return from their southern migration. Robins, Tree Swallows, and Bluebirds take up residence in the bird houses and rafters of the 22 buildings of the complex. In total, over 100 birds have been identified in the forests and fields of Wellington Farm USA.

Directions: Wellington Farm Park is south of Grayling, and north of Higgins Lake, on Military Road. Military Road runs north and south and is just a few miles west of U.S. 27 and I -75.

THE

SCENIC

BYWAY

IS A

POPULAR

ROUTE

TO

PARADISE

WHITEFISH BAY SCENIC BYWAY

The Whitefish Bay National Forest Scenic Byway makes for a great drive as part of a day trip, through the Hiawatha National Forest. The east end of the byway begins at the national forest boundary west of Brimley. At that point the roadway name changes from Lakeshore Drive, to Whitefish Bay Scenic Byway. The road follows the shoreline of Lake Superior most of the way. There are a few spots where it moves further inland into the forest. The west end of the byway is at the intersection with M-123, south of Paradise.

The drive winds through the forest and along the shoreline of Whitefish Bay. There are secluded beaches and great expanses of clear water. In the winter, the frozen lake is breathtaking, the forest is silent. A number of stops make the trip even more interesting. Just outside Brimley is Iroquois Point, and the Point Iroquois Lighthouse. During the summer season, the lighthouse is open. From the top one can see the Canadian shoreline across the lake.

Further west, the road runs along the shore of Tahquamenon Bay. For a short way it runs parallel with the North Country Trail. The trail crosses the road near Naomikong Creek, where travelers can stop, and enjoy the Naomikong Scenic Overlook. The drive continues west through pine and birch forests, all of it just, plain beautiful. The byway ends in the west at M-123. The whole thing from Sault Ste. Marie to M-123 is only about 30 miles and takes a couple hours with all of the stops. Turning north on M-123 will take you to Paradise. In Paradise you can pause for a bit. The Inn and Gastropub is a favorite stop of mine. They have a sandwich called the Log Splitter. It is one of the best brisket sandwiches I have ever eaten, mouth-watering hardly describes it. From Paradise it is only a short drive to either historic Whitefish Point, or the Tahquamenon waterfalls.

Directions: From Brimley To Route 123, go south on the Mackinac Trail out of Sault Ste. Marie to 6 Mile Road. Take 6 Mile Road west to Brimley where Lake Shore Drive begins.

WHITE PINE VILLAGE

Just outside of Ludington, Michigan is the Historic White Pine Village. The village depicts life in a small Michigan community of the late 1800s to the early 1900s. The complex sits on twenty three acres and is an especially good trip for kids. They can run off some of that energy in an educational venue. The intention of the village board is to provide *"an historical and educational experience for visitors in an atmosphere of nostalgia, serenity, and beauty"*. They have succeeded.

At this writing, the village has 29 buildings. Many are authentic historic structures, reflecting life in Mason county in pioneer times. The main building offers a short video that is worth watching. Then you take the self-guided tour through the village. The buildings are open and often have an audio playing that explains the exhibits in detail. There are thousands of artifacts and displays including a one room schoolhouse, chapel, blacksmith, music museum, and an ice cream parlor that still serves ice cream. In addition to these, the museum has two unique, rare exhibits.

One is an extremely rare electric Opera Car once owned by the Cartier family. An opera car has unusual design features. The front has a broad windshield. There is one bench seat in the front that goes all the way across the car. This seat was designed to accommodate the large skirts of evening gowns of the period. A lady could ride comfortably to the evening entertainment without wrinkling her gown. The driver sat in a single seat in the rear of the car and steered by means of a tiller, connected to a single rear wheel.

Gossip has a way of affecting a persons reputation, even years after the supposed event. Some said that Mrs. Cartier enjoyed taking the opera car for a spin or to go downtown shopping. Her driving skills were such that, when folks heard she was on the road, most people went inside since even the sidewalks were not considered safe.

Another unique feature of the village is Vintage Base Ball. Back in the day it was spelled with two words, base ball, and the rules were a bit different. A vintage base ball diamond has been set up in the northwest portion of the village. Players, called ballists believe it or not, put on period uniforms and play the game as it was originally meant to be played. The team known as The Ludington Mariners act as traveling ambassadors playing matches, games, at home at the village and across Michigan. They play by 1860 rules that are a bit different. Some "vintage" rules are, fielders do not use gloves, a fly ball caught on the first bounce is an out, the umpire doesn't call balls and strikes, and it is the duty of the pitcher to throw the ball so it's easy for the batter to hit it. By the way, the pitcher was called a Hurler and the batter a Striker.

There is a lot to take in at the Historic White Pine Village. It is definitely more than just a quick stop. The village is closed in the winter.

Directions: Ludington is on Lake Michigan about an hour and a half north of Grand Rapids. To get to the White Pine Village, take the Pere' Marquette Hwy. south 2 miles from the Mason County Airport, then west on Iris Road 1 ½ miles, then north ½ mile on South Lakeshore Dr.

WHITE

ROCK

WAS

AN

INFAMOUS

PHANTOM

TOWN

WHITE ROCK

There is a lot of history in Michigan that has been forgotten or lost. Route 25, along the Lake Huron shoreline, is often used by travelers to get to the Sanilac Petroglyphs or the Wilderness Arboretum in Port Austin. About half way up the thumb is the small town of White Rock. Folks usually notice the small lighthouse, but most don't know about the unique history of this place.

The name White Rock came about because of a huge white rock just offshore in Lake Huron. At one time it was quite large. It had served as a navigational aid, treaty boundary marker, and was considered a sacred place by Native Americans. That sacred status led to an event that has become more legend that factual account. The story goes that a group of settlers were having a celebration and decided to move the party out to the big white rock. They were warned against that action because the rock was sacred ground. All but one man ignored the advice. They moved out onto the rock and partied into the night. In the middle of the night a great lakes storm blew in and the group on the rock were caught in a lightning storm. Supposedly, a bolt of lightning struck the rock killing everyone there. The only survivor of that group was the man who stayed on shore.

White Rock was also one of the first "phantom towns" in Michigan. Immigrants were heading west. Those who traveled down the St. Lawrence Seaway, entered the Great Lakes, and would pause in Detroit. There they would arrange for overland transport, acquire supplies, and be presented with all manner of real estate opportunities. One of those was the vision for White Rock as the next great Michigan Metropolis. In hotel lobbies and saloons, real estate men showed immigrants a bright future in White Rock. They presented drawings and plans showing a fully platted city, with all necessary services including, police, hospital, and schools. The drawings depicted orderly improved streets with cleared lots, ready for development. Stories were told of booming commerce from lumber and harbor traffic on Lake Huron. Best of all, many of the choicest lots were still available at bargain prices and the town was only about 100 miles north. The town sold quickly since everybody loves a bargain.

When the buyers arrived in White Rock, they discovered that no town existed. There were no streets, no buildings, and no functioning harbor. In many cases the lots didn't even exist. The plat maps were fakes. The whole thing was a scam, a "phantom town". Many buyers hurried back to Detroit to try to recover their money, only to find that the sellers were long gone. The con men had headed west, to repeat the scam in Chicago and St. Louis. In the case of White Rock, the town was actually sold a of a number of times.

Eventually a small town grew up called White Rock, named for the big white rock, out there in the lake. The rock doesn't impress any longer. It has become rather small and ordinary. It wasn't due to wave erosion or any other natural cause. The huge white rock was used as a practice target to train bombers for World War II. Those guys became pretty accurate, eventually bombing the rock into smithereens. Only a small part of it remains.

LOST AND GONE

A friend who has passed away once said, "Things ain't what they once were and probably never was".

His point was that change is inevitable and through change some things are going to be lost. There are towns, destinations and artifacts that are nearly forgotten. Maybe a new highway bypassed the town, a 100 year old business shuts down, an attraction falls out of vogue. Soon, the stories about those places get lost in time, forgotten.

The Lost and Gone section in my books reminds us of some of those places. Some are still there, along the back road. Some are little more than a pile of ruins or are just a dim memory.

DOWLING GENERAL STORE - GONE

This destination is gone, though the building may still be there.

A relaxing drive, through the rolling hills of south central Michigan, can sometimes result in a step back in time. That is exactly what happens if you come across the Dowling General Store. Except for the addition of electricity and refrigeration, the Dowling General Store is very much like it was when it was established in 1864. The exterior is still white clapboard with large windows facing the main road and the ornate facade topping off the front of the second story. This is an old country store and they try to use locally grown ingredients for the wonderful baked goods they make. It is very likely that you will see Amish horse and buggy rigs parked here, while the farmers deliver fresh produce.

The first thing you will notice when you go in the store, is the fantastic aroma that fills the air. The bakery is famous in these parts, for the mouth-watering baked goods they offer up every day. Donuts and cookies are the favorites. I can tell you that a simple cinnamon donut here, fresh from the oven of course, is a taste delight to be savored. The only problem is that you may eat them, all of them, on the way before you can get home. Once you get over the first impact of the delicious smells you can enjoy the atmosphere. Baked goods in glass cases, old, old hardwood floors, home-made ice cream, and a couple of simple tables.

You can linger for conversation and a game of checkers, or just wander around and admire all of the antiques and artifacts from by gone days. There are a few dry goods available. Some fishing gear if you are headed for one of the nearby lakes, and fish stories, in case you don't have one of your own.

There are wonderful tales, from the history of the store. The Dowling General Store has served as a gathering place for the locals and as a refreshing pause for travelers since it was built. Back in the day, the second floor served as a dance hall, among other things, and was a big hit on Saturday nights. The second story of the store is closed at this time, but that doesn't mean it is unoccupied. For many years there have been encounters with "Howard" the ghost. Some say he used to live up there and some say he was a visitor who never missed a chance to cut a rug, at the Saturday night hoedowns. It doesn't matter which story you go with. People from all over keep running into

Howard. Sometimes he is in the store and sometimes he is outside. Sometimes there is just the sound of someone dancing away, late at night, in the old dance hall upstairs.

Another story, based on historical fact, is about the old tunnel. It seems that some years ago, the hardwood floors on the main level were buckling and had generally become less level. Folks decided to check the foundations in the basement, and during that inspection, discovered alcoves hidden behind the walls. Further investigations revealed that, at one time, The Dowling General Store was an important stop on the "Underground Railroad". The alcoves were secret places where refugees could hide and rest. While looking into the foundation issues, they also discovered the location of the old tunnel that used to lead under the road, to a house on the other side. It is said that a doctor owned that house, and when travelers on the underground railroad needed medical attention, the doctor could make his way through the tunnel, treat those in need, and return to his home without anyone being able to detect the hiding places under the store.

Directions: Dowling is about 15 minutes north of Battle Creek, Michigan on Route 37. The store is at the junction of 37 and the Dowling Rd.

SPIKEHORN - GONE

This destination is gone, only a ruin remains.

Growing up in rural Michigan in the late 1940s and early 1950s was a different life from today. Communities were smaller, distances seemed greater and paved roads were only found in the towns. Families were usually supported by one salary, often by the father who put in his shift at the factory. One of the most anticipated rituals of the time was the two-week summer vacation, and for many, that meant driving up past Clare where that magical land was found, "Up North". From the Lansing area, you would use U.S. 27. That was a two-lane paved "highway" that ran from Ohio to the straits of Mackinac. In those years, the road ended at the straits. Getting to the upper peninsula meant taking the car ferry. That could be a slow process and, during deer season, resulted in traffic backups that still live in legend. Along the way there were a few towns and a handful of attractions known as "tourist traps". On the roadside, near Harrison, was where you would find Spikehorn.

Born on July 15, 1870 his given name was John Meyers. Like most men in those days, he tried his hand at many trades as conditions required. At one point, they say he worked in one of the old coal mines near Williamston, Michigan. "They" say that was when he began talking about heading "Up North" to follow his dreams. At some point he did it, making his way to Harrison, Michigan, though he never learned to drive. Driving wasn't so much a necessity back then, U.S. 27 wasn't all that drivable at that time anyway. He started a small wildlife sanctuary and for the last thirty years of his life he was known far and wide as "Spikehorn".

My first memory of Spikehorn was in 1956 or 57 during a trip to Indian River. It was part of the ritual when we went up north to stop at "Spikehorns". I was 6 years old and it is a memory that remains fresh in my minds eye. It was early in the morning, we always traveled early. The ground was wet with dew and there was a foggy mist hanging in the pines. We kids followed the grownups into the old fenced in enclosure. As little ones, all adults seemed big, but when Spikehorn appeared for the first time, with a raccoon in his arms, it was like encountering a giant. He was a great blustery man with a booming voice and a massive white beard. He scared the pants off me. We wandered through the cages looking at the foxes and porcupines as he told my father tall tales in that booming voice and then, there they were, the bears. The giant mythical man walked right into their cage and hugged those bears. The black bear Bruno weighed in at over 600 pounds but seemed smaller in my eyes than gnarly old Spikehorn. He scared the pants off me.

I only remember a few other details. His little wildlife refuge was a ramshackle affair on the side of the road. He had whitetail deer, porcupines, foxes and the bears that would make him famous. By the time he made it into the press, travelers had already spread the legend of the wild man up north. He was the subject of a feature in the Detroit Free Press in 1931. As always, the bears with names like Nip, Tuck, Stub and Bruno, nearly stole the show. The animals were kept in natural surroundings and received loving care. There are no places like this anymore and no characters like Spikehorn, and it is unlikely there ever will be again. The ruins of the old roadside attraction are at the junction of Old 27 and Route 61 just outside Harrison, Michigan.

NOTES

NOTES

NOTES